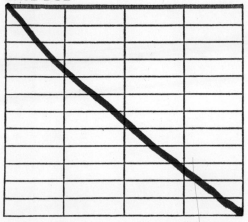

# Commuting Versus Resident Students

## Overcoming the Educational Inequities of Living Off Campus

# Arthur W. Chickering

FOREWORD BY ALEXANDER W. ASTIN

# Commuting Versus

# Resident Students

Jossey-Bass Publishers
San Francisco · Washington · London · 1974

*The*
*Jossey-Bass Series*
*in Higher Education*

# *Foreword*

$T$his major national study of residential living appears at a particularly opportune time in the history of higher education. In contrast to the early 1960s, when generous federal and state subsidies stimulated a dramatic expansion in residential facilities on college campuses, the past few years have been characterized by major cutbacks in dormitory construction, as well as by increasing ambivalence within the higher education establishment about the usefulness of college dormitories. Arthur Chickering's study raises fundamental questions about the wisdom of these recent trends.

Chickering's research is especially important in that it is an attempt to use technically sophisticated research methods to examine an array of problems that have traditionally been resolved on the basis of political considerations, economic constraints, or the prevailing educational folklore. While his answers are by no means the final word, Chickering's data suggest strongly that significant benefits accrue to students who go away from home to attend college. While he does not attempt to resolve the question of whether these "benefits" justify the additional "costs" of living away from home, perhaps his research may stimulate economically oriented researchers to undertake such a cost-benefit analysis. The results could be extremely useful for the development of educational policy in the future.

One would hope that these findings would also stimulate social scientists to take a close look at alternative modes of residential experiences. While it is clearly important to know that going away from home to live in a college residence tends to produce positive educational results, it is equally important to be able to know how to structure the residential experience in order to maximize these benefits. The possible research topics seem to be almost limitless: staffing, programing, roommate assignments, governance, and even architectural design of residential facilities.

Chickering's general conclusion that residential campus living positively affects student development takes on special significance when viewed in the light of his other major finding: that highly able and affluent students are much more likely to live in a dormitory during the college years than are the less able and less affluent students. These two findings suggest that the concepts of equal access and equality of educational opportunity need to be expanded to include access to residential facilities during the undergraduate years. Clearly, any student who, because of admissions requirements or economic constraints, is denied access to residential facilities does not have an educational opportunity equal to that of students who are able to live in dormitories.

In short, this pioneering study suggests that institutions that are currently considering abandoning their residential facilities might want to take a second look at the possible educational value of such facilities. Moreover, institutions that have dropped residence requirements and those considering dropping them may want to reexamine their policies in light of these results. Finally, at a higher policy level, state and federal legislators might be well advised to reconsider the current trend toward expansion of commuter colleges and withdrawal of support for construction of collegiate residences.

ALEXANDER W. ASTIN
*Cooperative Institutional Research
Program of the American
Council on Education and
the University of California,
Los Angeles*

# *Preface*

$M$y explicit concern with the impact of college on student learning and development began in 1959, when I assumed responsibility for evaluating an experiment in college curriculum organization carried out by Goddard College with the support of the Ford Foundation. That experiment, conceived and implemented from 1958 until 1965, by Tim Pitkin, George Beecher, Forest Davis, Robert Mattuck, and other members of the Goddard faculty and administration, tested and demonstrated the value of many of the "new" approaches spreading through higher education during the 1970s—individual independent study and "group independents," programed learning, use of work situations, volunteer activities and other experiences on and off campus as integrated and credited elements of the academic program, narrative evaluations, individually designed programs of study, and majors. (See Beecher, Chickering, and others, 1966; Chickering, 1969.) That experiment also indicated the powerful contribution to personal development and intellectual competence made by residence on a college campus, and substantial research during and since that period further documents that contribution. (See, for example, De Coster, 1967; Dressel and Lehmann, 1965; Heath, 1968; Katz and associates, 1968; Morishima, 1966; Newcomb, 1962, 1968; Vreeland and Bidwell, 1965; Wallace, 1966.) The problem of funding, constructing, and maintaining college residences and the role of the residential experience have become much more complex since the early sixties, and that complexity plus my own continuing interest prompted the commuter-resident studies that lie behind this book.

From the time of my early studies at Goddard, I have been committed to evaluating the implications of research for educational practice. That commitment has been reinforced by personal experiences as a researcher, by manifold evidence that the results of social science research are seldom seriously taken into account by educational decision-makers, and by my recent experiences as a college administrator.

This book aims to increase the chances that the results of research and the recommendations concerning commuting and resident students will be seriously considered and will influence the course of higher education. These studies have implications for administrators and faculty members in both public and private institutions who must provide the best education possible with the limited dollars available and who must make decisions concerning new educational programs and the residential facilities that are or are not called for as part of those programs. The results also have implications for legislators and legislative committees and for higher education administrators concerned with statewide planning and with developing new alternatives for the 1970s and 1980s. To make the research results reported here accessible to all these users, I summarize findings in simple, jargon-free language, deleting elaborate presentation of supporting evidence and omitting detailed discussions of data collection procedures and analytic methods. Brevity, clarity, and punch are called for.

But simple accessibility is not enough. The results and the recommendations must pertain to the major social and educational changes underway and to the decisions required by those changes. That pertinence is made clear here through general principles and concrete practical suggestions which are consistent with the findings and which recognize the constraints within which action must be taken.

The first chapters of this book speak to the basic social and educational issues, commenting on major social changes, on the new students coming into higher education as a consequence of these changes, and on the responses of higher education to these new students. A large body of literature is associated with each of these major areas, and the comments offered in these chapters do not pretend full coverage but rather sketch a general background. The remaining chapters then present the major findings, discuss basic educational and developmental principles, and offer recommendations to those in existing institutions and to those developing new approaches to higher education.

The research for this book and some of the writing were accomplished while I was a visiting scholar with the Office of Research of the American Council on Education during the 1970–1971 academic year. Most of the findings rest on freshmen surveys and follow-up questionnaires administered by the Office of Research from 1965 through 1970 and on a special survey carried out for the Carnegie Commission on Higher Education. Some findings also are reported from analyses carried out in the context of the Project on Student Development in Small Colleges, which was supported by a five-year grant from the National Institute of Mental Health. The results of the studies reported here have been corroborated by subsequent analyses of more recent data—analyses carried out by Alexander Astin and his staff at UCLA. Various references cited in the Bibliographic Commentary report research and theory which consistently support the general interpretation and the recommendations based on them.

Many of these analyses were carried out for students who live in various types of off-campus housing—apartments, rooming houses, and the like—as well as for students who live at home. Thus these two different groups of commuters can be compared with each other as well as with their residential peers.

The research, from beginning to end, was a collaborative effort. Without the active assistance, judicious intervention, and patient explanations of Alexander Astin and his staff, I would have fallen whimpering before bits of data which outnumber the sands of the Sahara or would have become hopelessly and helplessly entangled in computer tapes which stretch from here to eternity. Unassisted, I would never have dispelled the mysteries of the Creager Cell File and Stratification Design in a mere ten months. Solitary scholarship would never have resolved the differences among part, partial, parcel—parcel???—and zero order correlation coefficients, nor would single-handed efforts have revealed how much a beta weight weighs. Even after a year I noticed that many staff meetings still lapsed into Greek.

The Office of Research provided three other major sources of assistance. Jeanne Royer typed mountains of tables and manuscript, and handled a constant flow of mail and telephone calls. Ellen Kuper plowed through piles of print-outs, converting numbers into meaningful tables, summarizing the tables in her own words, and adding numerous insights and interpretations from her own experiences. And Jerry Richardson, who can make the most complicated computer jump through hoops, bailed out major analyses that seemed irrevocably lost or infinitely delayed.

Finally, there was the daddy of them all, the Council itself, its administrative staff and leadership. The Council provided a salary coupled with attractive and comfortable facilities conveniently located. Most important, it allowed, with only a slightly bemused tolerance, a somewhat deviant character from the woods of Vermont to ride the elevators, climb the stairs, and walk the halls without prejudice or embarrassment.

Most of the writing and preparation of the final draft have been done in bits and pieces of time squeezed out since I assumed an administrative position to help get a new educational venture, Empire State College, underway—a situation hardly conducive to long periods of uninterrupted reading, reflection, and writing or to freedom from powerful preoccupation with a wide range of problems that, to say the least, are nonacademic. But these experiences have added a perspective that would have been otherwise absent. A crash month in a garden house made available by Nancy Edwards on beautiful Lake Amatitlan in Guatemala, occasional brief stretches in the woods of Vermont, and substantial assistance from John McCormick finally got the job finished. Now that it is done, I can more fully appreciate the patience and forbearance of Sandy Astin and the staff of the American Council on Education during the time I spent in their stimulating and pleasant environs.

This book is dedicated to my wife, Jo, whose knowledge, insights, and experiences continually enrich my work and my life, and whose perspectives, good humor, and affection have sustained me during the years this effort was underway.

*East Montpelier, Vermont*
*September 1974*

ARTHUR W. CHICKERING

# Contents

# Commuting Versus Resident Students

## Overcoming the Educational Inequities of Living Off Campus

# The New
# Society

*Higher* education today must respond to the challenges posed by three major conditions. Rapid social changes are forcing redefinition of the role of colleges and universities and of the college degree. Increased numbers of students with diverse motivations are adding their special educational needs and purposes to those of the typical students of the past. The costs of traditional alternatives are outrunning the support for them.

As these conditions emerged a decade ago the response of higher education was simple expansion. Private institutions undertook major new construction. State systems started new colleges and universities and expanded existing ones, copying with only minor wrinkles the models of the past. Community colleges came on the scene in large numbers. But with a few exceptions, although presented with new kinds of students and their special relationships to the communities, the same basic procedures, facilities, and approaches to teaching and learning that had characterized four-year colleges and universities since the turn of the century were adopted. In short, the response of higher education to the new social conditions and new students of the 1960s was more of the same.

Residential arrangements are a case in point. During the late

**1**

1950s and 1960s, spurred by low interest federal loans, major building programs increased dramatically the dormitory space available for the rapidly growing college population. Today, under the guns of inflation and rising costs, of decreasing federal and foundation support, and of decelerating tax support, many state and many private institutions have ceased or sharply curtailed new construction and are looking toward new nonresidential approaches to higher education. The cumulative effect of these individual decisions has been steady and rapid increases in the proportions of commuting students.

These decisions were made in the light of clear and detailed evidence concerning the costs of building, maintaining, and staffing college residences, but without analyses of the educational benefits that accrue from those facilities. Now, however, major social changes are demanding changes in higher education, and one major change concerns college residences, the residential experience, its place in and contribution to higher education. But decisions for change have been consistent with the general all-or-nothing approach which has characterized U.S. higher education until very recently.

Colleges and universities tend to be either residential or commuter. A student has a choice between two alternatives. If he chooses a residential college, he commits himself to an institution which expects him to live in college housing or a fraternity or sorority nine months of each year for four years. If he chooses a commuter college, he lives at home or finds an apartment from which he goes to class and returns for nine months of each year for four years. Usually the only difference between the residential college and the commuting college is that one has extensive dormitory facilities and the other does not. Some commuting colleges respond to the special problems of their students by investing in lounges, offering more courses during evening and weekend hours, providing large parking spaces, running buses from central locations accessible to public transportation. But there are no significant responses to the special backgrounds of many commuting students, no attempts to deal with the difficulties they have in discovering and connecting with academic programs and extracurricular activities suitable to them, and no solutions to the difficulties they face in building new relationships with students and faculty members and with the institution itself.

And there has been no serious testing of new arrangements which might let commuters participate in residential experiences and receive the educational benefits that can flow from them. The simplistic solution of eliminating the residential facilities and maintaining essentially the same educational programs and processes has resulted in major differences in the college experiences and educational benefits for commuters and residents. These differences will persist until thoughtful analyses and significant changes address the problem. This totalistic swing, if it continues, will have serious consequences for the meaning of higher education and for its contribution to society, especially during a period of social change, when effective higher education for increasing numbers of diverse students is more and more necessary.

In the agrarian communities and urban ghettos which preceded the technological revolution, a man lived his life among interpersonal, social, and environmental relationships which indicated who he was and where he was going. The community was stable. The cobweb of interactions was single and integrated. Work, family, friends, worship, recreation, learning, and social obligations were fused. There was little diversity in occupations, values, religious orientations, racial or ethnic backgrounds. Communication with others, though with a limited range of persons, was constant and patterned.

The traditional residential college where students came to live for large blocks of time, for four or more years, was a consistent and natural extension of the stable, internally homogeneous, and cohesive community from which they came. In this residential situation, this college community, this community of scholars and students, each student met others who were from similar backgrounds and who were making a similar transition to an adult community almost as predictable and stable as the one from which they came. Through gradual processes of mutual selection they found roommates, hallmates, and others, who were compatible; they created relatively closed and stable friendship groups with whom they spent most of their time. This dynamic reached its extreme expression in the fraternities and sororities that worked carefully at the processes of selection and which brought "brothers" and "sisters" together in closed living situations for three or more years—systems guided by stable and clearly defined prescriptions for behavior, values, roles, and future aspirations.

Thus the traditional residential college provided a fitting transition from the childhood and adolescent life of a stable small town community, to the larger life of an adult job, home, and family which would be relatively fixed and enduring. It put a premium on getting along and fitting in, on adapting to the givens of the college community, the residence hall, the fraternity or sorority. The person who came out of those experiences successfully was ready to fit into the job, the house, the family, the church, the Rotary Club, Chamber of Commerce, the Masons. This fitting in was made possible by the continuous and rich flow of information and understandings mediated by an integrated college culture and climate in which the residential student was immersed twenty-four hours a day. If there was a reasonably good fit between the characteristics he came with and those valued by the institution, the transition was smooth; the student found his way to those academic and extracurricular activities that suited his interest and abilities without much difficulty. He heard about teachers and courses from other students and observed directly their excitement or boredom, successes and failures. He took time to sniff around and to test out relationships with various individuals and groups until he found those that were appealing and that would accept him. Once accepted, the frequent and intense associations let him move to full and respected membership quickly.

But that model of long term close living with like minded peers no longer suits the student of today. Major social changes have created conditions that are sending a new and diverse array of students on to post-secondary education. Since World War II there has been both an explosion in numbers and in the cultural, economic, and ethnic backgrounds among students seeking admission to, and success through, the two-year and four-year colleges and universities of the United States. Furthermore, just as the industrial revolution created an adolescence where none existed before, these social changes create a new development period—youth, or the young adult that is different from adolescence and different from the maturity that came with the stability of fixed occupational, familial, and community roles and responsibilities. In addition, the major shift in the center of gravity from survival and production to self-realization and self-expansion, alters conceptions concerning individual development during the middle years and after and creates new constituencies for higher education. Today's students do not need to learn how to fit into a stable situation; they need to learn how to create and re-create their own identities as they encounter diverse subcultures that call for diverse roles, values, appearances, behaviors. They belong simultaneously to many groups and to diverse networks of social relationships. Language, actions, and values suitable for one situation may not be for another.

Now community is no longer given. Each person has to create his own and to carry it around inside himself, nurture it, keep it alive. Consequently, there has developed much greater self-consciousness about community characteristics, interest groups, subcultures, how to find them, and how to gain access. Now, in much more self-conscious fashion, we create our own networks of friendships and reference groups; we expand and diversify the communities we build into ourselves; we take charge of our own development—developing interpersonal competence and tolerance for those who differ, clarifying our purposes, testing our independence and areas of interdependence, developing our own frameworks for belief and behavior which can be held with integrity.

Basically, man has a fundamental impulse toward and need for re-creation, self-expansion, self-development. Today, fundamental changes in population and human contact, in generating information, in the exchange of human knowledge and experiences, in energy and work create fundamental changes in human existence, human requirements, and human development. The consequence of these changes is a fundamental shift in the core of human existence. A new center of gravity for human purposes is replacing that organizing force which has driven man since he crawled from the sea or was banished from Eden.

Two major motors have powered human lives, two major purposes have been the poles by which individuals charted their time and energy—survival and re-creation. During the early stages of human existence the overwhelming concern was survival. Most of the daylight and much of the darkness were spent obtaining or creating food, clothing, and shelter. There was time to draw on the cave, to carve a fine tool handle of wood or bone, to weave colored strands and original designs into the linsey-woolsey of daily existence. There was time for periodic celebrations, rituals, and religious observances. But time for these re-creational activities was limited. Simple survival overwhelmed all else.

In time, as man became more skilled in managing his environment, as social organizations grew, as agricultural practices developed, as industrial and technological advances occurred, the minimum requirements were more readily obtained, and man worked for increasing comfort and security. This work has been highly successful. In the United States and in much of the Western Hemisphere north of the equator, most men have more than adequate food, clothing, and shelter; most men have quite comfortable and secure lives. Since World War II, for more and more persons, comfort and security have meant conspicuous consumption and keeping up with the Joneses—an extra television set, a second car, a boat, a bigger house, perhaps even a little home in the country.

But conspicuous consumption soon leads to diminishing returns because each acquisition reduces the significance of the next. We stave off boredom by turning toward sensuality. Fancy eating becomes a big thing; cocktails and creative hors d'oeuvres before dinner, followed by new dishes from abroad with appropriate wines, topped off by an elegant dessert and perhaps a dram of Drambuie. Sexual relationships become more flexible and free so we can more frankly devote greater time, energy, and resources to such pursuits. Sauna baths, skiing, and vacations in the sun also help. Drugs open a new world where many hours can be spent. But the problem is that the senses get satisfied. They give transitory relief and renewal, but no lasting answers; and some sources of satisfaction, if too relentlessly pursued, become self-destructive. In short, acquiring food, clothing, shelter, and their recent extensions into comfort, conspicuous consumption, and sensuality are no longer lasting or sufficient purposes. They no longer provide a fulfilling core for our existence. We cannot ignore those needs, but for a meaningful life they no longer can be given top priority.

For the first time in human existence priority can be given to re-creation. For the first time, a culture can shift its priorities so that not simply a small elite, but the masses of its members, can organize their lives around the search for new experiences, new challenges, new opportunities which will stimulate and enable their continued self-expansion and self-development. Food, clothing, shelter, and creature comforts must still be provided, but they no longer need consume prime time and energy; they no longer need be the anchor for human existence.

Major changes are underway in the world of work, changes that are reorganizing that world so that recreational and educational activities can be more effectively pursued. Industry is moving away from the atomistic assembly line approach where time and motion studies emphasize efficiency through economies of effort and movement and through repetition of simply-managed small tasks. Now systematic efforts to provide job enrichment are being tested. Even high wages do not, in the long run, compensate for an existence where challenge, variety, and re-creation are precluded. As the cultural shift underway continues, job candidates will not only think about salary, fringe benefits, and retirement plans, but will seriously ask a new series of questions: What kinds of competence will this work foster? What new points of view or new ideas will I encounter? What new concepts and understandings will I have to master? What different kinds of persons will I meet and have to work with?

There are similar cultural shifts underway in marriage, family living, and definitions of community. The Sawyer family lives about a mile through the woods from our house in East Montpelier, Vermont, a town of 1300. They still milk by hand, haul wood, plow and hay with horses, and walk a mile to the general store on the blacktop to get their food. They have not been to Burlington, a city of 40,000 forty miles away, in the eight years we have been neighbors, and I do not know whether they have ever been out of the state. They have a television set and read the Times-Argus, published in Barre, population 13,000, eight miles away. As children they walked to a one-room school where they met boys and girls whose parents ran nearby farms or an occasional shop. They spent six to eight years in that school with those fellow students and then quit to pick up the work on the family farm.

The Robinsons also live in East Montpelier. Mr. Robinson went to public schools in Massachusetts through grade ten when difficulties arising from parental divorce sent him off to private school for grades eleven and twelve. After high school the army took him around eastern United States and to the beaches, bars, and barrios of Rio de Janeiro. He was bounced out of the University of New Hampshire and let into a university in Connecticut on probation, from which he graduated with his own independently fashioned program which included two summers in Europe.

Mrs. Robinson was born in California and moved to Massachusetts when she was a child. She attended two different colleges while obtaining her undergraduate degree and four different graduate schools while obtaining her master's degree. During the first seven years of their marriage, Mr. and Mrs. Robinson and their four young children lived in five different communities in New Jersey and New York. Summers were spent in New Hampshire and winter weekends were spent racing to Vermont for skiing and camping. During the next thirteen years, they lived in four different communities in three different states. During the last two of those years, Mr. and Mrs. Robinson lived in New York. Their teenage children chose to remain in Vermont, and Mr. and Mrs. Robinson visit them on weekends and during holidays.

But if Mr. and Mrs. Robinson's life contrasts with the Sawyers', consider the Robinsons' four children at ages eighteen, sixteen, fourteen, and thirteen. They have lived in Manhattan, Long Island, New Jersey, Maryland, and Vermont. They have lived in the city, the suburbs, and on a farm where the neighbor is a mile away, where the only visible houses are five miles across the valley, and where they have a two-and-a-half mile walk to the school bus. Three different family camping trips have taken them to every state in the union and to eastern and western Canada. In pairs they have taken separate trips with their grandmother or mother to western Europe and Greece.

During the summer of his seventeenth year, the oldest, a boy, hitchhiked from Vermont to Cincinnati and back to help a girl who had run away from home. He entered college at eighteen and moved into a run-down, beat-up, cheap, cubbyhole apartment deep in a large city and began work with a grass-roots community agency helping minority group persons cope with prison, poverty, and lack of education. During the summer of her sixteenth year the oldest girl bicycled through three states and drove to various locations in the northeast on bicycle trips and races. That same summer the two younger girls traveled three hundred miles to a gymnastics camp where they were joined by others from around the country for intensive training by former Olympic competitors.

That is what the statistics on social change come down to. The meaning of community and its impact on the existence and personal development of the Sawyers, on Mr. and Mrs. Robinson, and on their children has shifted dramatically in a generation and a half.

The problem is to achieve and to maintain some self-consistency while moving through diversity, to maintain equilibrium while being continually pushed off balance by the insistent forces that penetrate each life. There are several ways to maintain self-consistency and equilibrium. Some alternatives—alienation and withdrawal, rigid self-sealing, selective perception, and cognitive gymnastics which convert discordant information into acceptable form—stall personal development if pursued too long. Development continues when students have the capacity for other alternatives: when they can recognize the different behaviors and values called for, when they have the personal strength to make their own choices, and when they have the experiences and skills to modify their own attitudes and behaviors accordingly.

Most persons continually push toward both greater diversity and greater unity. If higher education is to help, it must create the conditions to allow and foster this dynamic. Three basic conditions foster such development: varied direct experiences and roles, meaningful achievement, and relative freedom from anxiety and pressure.

Colleges, and current trends in higher education, offer particularly powerful opportunities for creating the conditions for a new start in relative anonymity, where some of the limiting expectations of other associations can be set aside or questioned. They offer exposure to a wide variety of life styles, values, concepts, and information, through group experiences, independent studies, work, volunteer activities, field experiences, and travel, systematically built into academic programs. They offer an increasingly diverse array of students and faculty members, who are different in age, ethnic, economic, intellectual, and geographic backgrounds. But these potentials are activated only if colleges become self-conscious about them and help students do the same.

Residential experiences have much to contribute to these

basic experiences. The most potent learning occurs in situations where persons come to know each other fully. Effective and affective exchange requires going beyond the persona to the person, behind the presented self to the self. Most of us know from experiences with weekend workshops, week long retreats, boat trips, camping expeditions, and the like that residential experiences foster that kind of knowing efficiently and effectively. It happens in college residences, and it is no accident that research indicates that most changes in attitudes, values, future plans and aspirations, and intellectual interests at college occur during the first and second years, as resident students come to grips with fellow students and college subcultures. We also know that requiring students to spend large blocks of time in college dormitories throughout their college career makes little educational sense. The evidence is clear that the impact and value of those residence hall experiences tapers off rather rapidly after the first or second year.

But the proper response is not the complete elimination of residential experiences, not the development of more commuter colleges. The results of the research reported in this book, and of other pertinent research, clearly document the substantial limitations in the academic, extracurricular, and interpersonal experiences and activities of commuting students and the relative advantages of residential students in these same areas. These results also document substantial differences in educational outcomes and personal development, outcomes that increase the gap between the commuters and residents already apparent as entering freshmen and that have long range consequences for their future plans and aspirations and for their conceptions of themselves as citizens and as mature adults. The proper response, therefore, is thoughtful development of new arrangements which make residential experiences part of the fabric of education and which make them available to all students, not just to an affluent minority. New residential arrangements will make a difference, but other changes are needed to help the student begin more effectively and plan and carry out a sound program once that beginning is made. Therefore, new approaches to admissions, orientation and program planning, to curriculum and teaching, and to available learning resources, also must be tested.

And unless more is done than simply trading the totalism of

the ivory tower residential institution for the totalism of the streetcar college, then many of the most significant contributions of higher education will be lost. Colleges and universities must respond not only to these major social changes under way, but also to the educational needs of these new young adults and adults, and to the developmental potentials open to them.

# 2

# The New Students

*T*here are three major groups of today's students whose backgrounds have not been typical of college students in the past. Foremost among these, in terms of numbers, are young persons from lower socioeconomic levels with poor academic records. Few of these students entered college during the fifties and early sixties, but now more than half those that enter plan to continue. Cross, on the basis of her own research and that of others, describes them well (1972, pp. 11–13):

> The majority of them are the white sons and daughters of blue-collar workers, although a significant number are from ethnic minorities. Two-thirds are first generation college students; their parents have had no experience with college. These young people do not read much outside of school. They prefer to spend their time watching television, rapping with friends, or creating things with tools for the boys or cooking and sewing for the girls. When New Students are asked what they do best, they mention talents that are not developed in school, whereas traditional students are most likely to select activities such as reading or working with numerical con-

cepts. Thus I conclude that these New Students have been unlikely to find rewards for good performance within the school system. If they want praise and even self-respect, they will probably have to find it elsewhere. It is not surprising then that these students are vocationally oriented and are attending college to get the credentials that lead to better jobs. They don't seek intellectual stimulation from their classes, nor do they anticipate discovering the joy of learning; they just hope to survive and to protect themselves against too obvious failure. Statistically, only 16 percent of these New Students score in the top one-third on the Intellectual Disposition Scale of the Omnibus Personality Inventory compared to 60 percent of the traditional students that higher education was designed to serve.

But these New Students don't blame the school system for their lack of success; unfortunately, they blame themselves. They are basically conservative young people who believe in the puritan work ethic. Broadly speaking, they respect the authority of the school and the state, and they believe that hard work is the way to get ahead and that people get what they deserve in this life. Many of them are already working at part-time jobs both because they need the money and, I suggest, because they need the psychological boost that working at a job gives them. There is some evidence to indicate that they learn job-related material well because it is usually concrete and its usefulness is apparent.

A second group of new students are those from inner city streets, variously termed disadvantaged, culturally deprived, underprepared, high risk, who are entering college through special preparatory programs and through diverse open admissions arrangements. Descriptions of the disadvantaged student vary. A typical description defines such students as those who, in addition to scoring poorly on standardized achievement tests, have experienced economic deprivation, social alienation caused by racial or ethnic discrimination, geographic isolation or provincialism. Other descriptions suggest that such persons feel powerless to control their lives, lack self-esteem and achievement motivation, have little vocational direction or sense of purpose, and have a negative self-image. These students are of no single race, color, religion, or ethnic background. They come from an inner city or from parts of the country that are rich in their own traditions but that do not prepare them for school or to operate successfully in society. They bring their cultural backgrounds and mores to college and find that they are misunderstood, rejected, ridiculed, or ignored. Adversary relationships quickly develop.

Many of the disadvantaged are women: waitresses, clerks, nurse's aids, cleaning women, barmaids, unwed mothers, deserted wives. A surprising number have the sole responsibility for supporting one or more children and maintaining a household. The disadvantaged men in college outnumber the women almost three to one. except for black men and women where the ratio is probably about reversed. The man usually dresses better but often may not be as responsible as his female counterpart. He procrastinates and dissipates more. He will occasionally have had minor scrapes with the police. He is self-sufficient and worldly. Some come directly from high school, others come from the service or from several years holding jobs and raising families.

The disadvantaged black student is usually quite different from the white student of the same class, and Moore (1970, pp. 49, 50) knows him well:

> To begin with the black student is more cynical. He does not believe in God, Mother, and Country with the same fervor as his white counterpart or his own parents. He is candid, not given to the little charades of guile. If he does not like a teacher, he does not pretend to like him. The black student has few heroes. He knows that society destroys its heroes even while it creates them; so he looks for the feet of clay earlier. He can probably take disappointments better, because in his world disappointment is a way of life. The black student will tend to be more worldly though less sophisticated academically. He shows much more ingenuity outside the classroom. Inside the classroom he has always been more of a spectator than a participant because he does not have a great deal of confidence in his ability. He considers the bits and

pieces of knowledge middle-class students verbalize as trivia used to show off.

The black student is probably more tolerant of injustice, stupidity, sarcasm, dirt, profanity, and illegitimacy. He chooses his leaders from among those who can best represent him. He is willing to listen and associate with students that school officials do not consider good citizens because he does not feel that association produces contamination. The black student does not confide in his parents. He will rarely let a teacher or a referee or some other arbiter handle the problem or confrontation between himself and another. He has been independent too long for that, and he has had to solve his own problems and often bear his own misfortune without assistance, sympathy, or compromise. Many of these students, especially those from lower socioeconomic environments, have been completely on their own since their early teens and have had to function as adults—in all of the dimensions of adulthood—while playing the role of children in school.

The basic point is that students from disadvantaged backgrounds have quite a wide array of positive characteristics, although these characteristics are not necessarily those required for success in an academic setting. Many such students are tough, resourceful, and self-reliant. They can generate creative solutions and concrete plans for action in response to complex problems when the situations have some pertinence to their own experiences. Many are strong competitors, want to learn and get ahead, and will work hard and take risks to develop competence and knowledge in those areas that are likely to pay off. They also often have a well tuned sensitivity to the attitudes and motives of others and to points of vulnerability and strength—and they have the ability to exploit those insights or not, as they see fit. Although inner city streets are tough teachers, fifteen or twenty years of daily instruction generate areas of competence, knowledge, and working experience unavailable to the farm boy or suburban youth. Obviously, there are also areas left untouched. Education in general, and higher education in particular, has been oriented toward the strengths of the middle and upper middle class, rural, small town, or suburban youth and has not had to worry about their weaknesses. Now higher education also must recognize the strengths, and not simply the weaknesses of students coming from blue-collar backgrounds and from the cities, if it is to respond to the social changes underway during the 1970s.

The number of adults pursuing some kind of further education also is increasing dramatically, soaring during the sixties from about nine million to twenty-five million. These increases are occurring among both men and women. Men moving into new employment and women resuming interrupted careers or pursuing delayed interests are seeking extension courses, correspondence studies, new degree programs, and numerous less institutionalized opportunities for education and in-service training. Although the rate of increase is greater for women than for men, the proportion of men is large, and the range of ages and backgrounds for both men and women is great. At Empire State College, a new "university without walls" under development as part of the State University of New York, the proportion of men has been consistently higher than 40 percent, ages range from the teens to the seventies with an average around thirty-five, and students come from all social classes and occupational backgrounds.

There is another array of new students, in addition to those above, whose backgrounds have not been typical of college students in the past. They come from the pool of middle and upper class high school graduates between the ages of sixteen and twenty-five who have been the primary constituents of the nation's colleges and universities until the early sixties. These students are "new" in their general maturity and in their orientations toward college, toward work, toward marriage and family life, and toward the place of education in their total existence. A small fraction are so alienated that they have withdrawn and turned their backs on the society and its institutions. Many more have not withdrawn but are bitter about the pattern of events in Indochina and Watergate, and are cynical about the establishment. They recognize, however, that effective influence calls for broad based competence and knowledge. They recognize that sound and workable solutions require many hours of homework together with pick-and-shovel efforts to obtain accurate information and to prepare persuasive cases which attract support

or compel action. They recognize that sheer idealism, even when
backed by powerful commitments, does not do the job.

Louis Benezet is president of the State University of New
York at Albany, an institution that serves large numbers of diverse
students and that has developed several innovative programs in
response to this diversity. He describes these new students this way
(*Chronicle of Higher Education,* November 20, 1972, p. 8):

> Student interest in university decision-making
> comes down, in concrete terms, to a demand for change
> in what is being taught in the general undergraduate pro-
> gram. Many students—just how many, we don't know—
> believe the big questions that will affect their lives in the
> world they face are not being tackled in the college courses.
>
> There is a growing expression of belief that tradi-
> tional liberal arts and science disciplines will not do the
> job for mankind, if we are to have a world worth living
> in by the year 2000, or perhaps if we are to have a world
> at all.
>
> What should one learn in college in order to help
> build a world of peace, social justice, and a tolerable en-
> vironment during the next thirty years? The colleges have
> said, "Learn what those before you learned: knowledge
> of man's history, his thought, and his creations; and
> knowledge of the make-up of the natural universe." To-
> day's students reply, "That's all right for professional
> scholars. It's not all right for those who want to do some-
> thing about society as matters are going now."
>
> Student interest in university decision-making
> focuses on a desire to change college studies more directly
> toward planning a better world. When faculty members
> point out that a center of learning cannot be at the same
> time a center of social policy, students ask, "Why not?"
>
> Massive student interest in environmental studies
> has prompted university developments of course sequences
> and majors. The University of Wisconsin at Green Bay,
> the University of California at Santa Barbara, and sev-
> eral others offer entire curricula in environmental educa-
> tion. Student pressures have led to new courses on the
> inner city, on ethnic studies, on peace studies, and on

women's studies. None of these came out of careful faculty deliberation in the way that the general education movement was started forty years ago or as area studies (Latin-American, Asian, American, Middle European) were begun ten to fifteen years ago. The current new courses have been born out of a student demand that managed to locate a sympathetic faculty response. To center such courses in the core of the undergraduate liberal arts program is the driving interest behind much of the current student activism.

These shifts in orientation and interests, like white caps spinning off a heavy ground swell, are only surface manifestations of more fundamental sea changes that have operated with special force during the precollege lives of today's middle and upper middle class students.

Prior to World War II there were few kindergartens and few children in them. By 1950, 77 percent of the students entering elementary school had attended some form of kindergarten and by 1970 the figure had reached 90 percent. In 1950 less than 10 percent of the children attended nursery school or prekindergarten programs, but in 1970, 37.5 percent of the 10.9 million persons in that age group were enrolled. Furthermore, the large numbers of children in day care centers and more or less organized play groups, are not included in those figures. On top of these earlier starts, better health, more effective bussing, and slightly longer school years have increased the average number of days per student in primary and secondary schools from 157 to 171 in the past twenty years. In addition to formal schooling, summer schools, summer camps, special institutes, or private instruction devoted to sports, travel, music, sciences, ecology, foreign languages have provided opportunities for additional learning, often with expert teachers, for students with special talents or for those students who want to explore further a tentative interest piqued in school or out. According to Ernest Boyer, chancellor of the State University of New York, "What all this adds up to is the little recognized fact that the eighteen-year-old today has spent roughly one-fourth more time in formal schooling than his counterpart twenty years ago, and twice as much as his grandparents did a half century ago" (1972, p. 9).

Qualitative changes have kept pace with these quantitative ones. Elementary school students now tackle advanced concepts in physics, math, and chemistry. They study Eskimo and Indian cultures with rich materials that allow for both cognitive and affective complexity that is a far cry from the cowboys and indians of the thirties. They take field trips, see films, listen to records, and meet resource persons who bring concepts from political science, economics, sociology, psychology, anthropology to life. Studies of foreign languages begin in junior high school if not before.

The high schools are changing with equal speed. Boyer recently reported the results of a survey by the State University of New York which showed the following changes in course enrollments in New York State between 1967 and 1970: "A 50 percent enrollment increase in fifth-year French, music theory, calculus, sculpture, and second-year American history; a 100 percent rise in students taking second-year physics, probability theory and statistics, plastics, photography, and Asian and African history; and a 200 percent jump in courses in astronomy, sociology, and comparative religion" (1972, p. 10). To put the frosting on the cake, these qualitative changes in content and complexity have occurred concurrently with a national drop in pupil-teacher ratio from 25.6 to 1 a decade ago to 22 to 1 today.

Not surprisingly, these quantitative and qualitative changes have produced high school graduates with academic competence and knowledge substantially beyond earlier generations. Standardized achievement test scores suggest that they are a year ahead of where their parents were at the same age, and several years ahead of the average student of the 1920s.

A shift to widespread knowledge of and access to good nutrition and health practices have had measurable consequences for physiological development. The average age for the onset of puberty has dropped from fourteen to twelve. The average height of both men and women has increased more than an inch, and full height is reached at age seventeen or eighteen instead of at nineteen or twenty. The average life span has increased dramatically and the working life span has more than doubled.

Basically, then, the industrial revolution of the nineteenth century and the technological revolution of the twentieth have had fundamental consequences for human development. In a brief period of a hundred years, without any assistance from any mutations, western man has amplified and accelerated his physiological and intellectual development and the social, emotional, and psychological concomitants associated with these fundamental areas. The increasing complexity of society and the exposure to that complexity through the mass media, the extension of public education through high school and college, the increased number and variety of jobs requiring specialized skills and training, the increased ease of travel and the easy access to diverse climates and cultures—all these new conditions have created a new developmental period for the young adult and new developmental potentials for older persons, never before available.

The basic dimensions of human development—competence, emotions, autonomy, identity, interpersonal relationships, purposes, integrity—have been elaborated in some detail in an earlier publication (Chickering, 1969) so they will not be spelled out here. It is significant to note, however, that these dimensions are the overarching framework within which the individual purposes of the new students entering higher education will be pursued. As colleges and universities respond, decisions must be anchored in two fundamental propositions. First, the range of diversity represented by both the "new students" who come from backgrounds not typical of college students in the past and the "new students" coming from typical middle and upper class backgrounds, must be met with equal diversity of content and process. Second, the alternatives for content and process must not only enable the pursuit of specific educational or vocational interests and goals, but must also help students of all ages pursue those major dimensions of human development that are most salient for them.

# 3

## The New
## Curriculum

*H*igher education today is responding to the social changes, the accompanying shifts in cultural priorities, and to the new students who bring new wants and needs, in three major ways: two-year colleges are undergoing explosive growth; traditional colleges and universities are changing; new nontraditional institutions are being developed.

Although enrollments continue to rise the rapid growth in numbers of institutions is leveling off. A recent report of the Carnegie Commission on Higher Education (1971) estimates that about 200 more strategically located institutions would put a community college within commuting distance of 95 percent of the population in the United States. Thus there is no question that during the last decade the two-year community college has been the most significant addition to higher education in this country.

Until recently the most distinguishing feature of the community college has been its open door policy for admission emphasising comprehensive education for the masses. This characteristic obviously implies a new educational philosophy accompanied by new processes as well as new content. Unfortunately few two-year colleges have met these commitments. Although new areas of content have been introduced most two-year institutions have adopted the educational procedures and physical arrangements of the four-year institutions that preceded them.

> Too often the term "open door" is hypocritical rhetoric. It is a catch phrase which implies every student can enroll in the college. Open door means more than the idea that every student with a high school diploma can go to college. It also means that the student, regardless of his level of achievement, will receive the best education possible in the college commensurate with his needs, efforts, motivation, and abilities. In reality, however, most community colleges develop the traditional programs and curricula which prepare able students to transfer to the senior institution, or terminal students to go directly into employment. The overwhelming majority of two-year institutions neither develop the same commitment, establish the same priorities nor utilize the same precision and creativity in developing the programs and curricula for the educationally disadvantaged student as they do for the able student. This student is one of the academically overlooked—or, perhaps, ignored. Disregard for the marginal student is one of the provocative footnotes that demonstrate the inability of higher education to come to terms in dealing with the nontraditional college student. In this way, post-secondary education has made little or no attempt to manage change or to match the prevailing needs with the times [Moore, 1970, p. 5].

Although enrollments in the community colleges will continue to grow—predictions suggest more than four million full and half-time students by 1980—the seventies will be a period when more attention must be given to effective program development. The report of Project Focus, a Kellogg Foundation supported study of the long range goals of the nation's community and junior colleges, suggests some of the areas that will receive attention (Bushnell and Zagaris, 1972):

1. Continued support for the concept of the open door will require more effective developmental education program offerings. Tested alternatives directed at both strengthening the student's

learning skills and motivation will be needed. Faculty members will require radically improved pre- and in-service training if they are to effectively meet the needs of a diverse array of students.

2. Greatly expanded minority group enrollment will require dramatic increases in the number of minority group faculty representatives, counselors, and administrators. Expanded recruitment programs and in-service training are needed to help resolve the current imbalance.

3. Strengthened lifelong learning programs will require institutional commitments and appropriate staffing well beyond the current level. Budgetary procedures and administrative support mechanisms will need to overhauled to insure greater continuity of programing.

4. Improved ways of articulating career and transfer programs will need to be adopted if loss of credit is to be avoided. Clustered courses and core curricula will help to eliminate the separateness. Work study programs, part-time enrollment, intermittent enrollment, and external degrees offer promising alternatives to traditional procedures.

5. Closer linkage of the community with the college will be achieved through systematic assessment and communication. Off-campus course offerings, community involvement in policy making, television coverage of campus events, outreach recruiting will help to insure a close collaborative relationship between the community and the college.

6. New organizational structures will emerge which encourage those who should participate in decision-making to do so. The typical bureaucratic structure of the past with its hierarchical alignment of administrators, staff, and students will give way to a participatory management framework with both faculty and administrators serving as learning managers. A results-oriented set of goals and objectives will facilitate a more effective allocation of resources for the benefit of the student and the community.

Changes to meet these goals have been underway in the four-year colleges and are gaining increased momentum. In a study of undergraduate curriculum trends Dressel and DeLisle (1969) examined college catalogs published by a random selection of 322 undergraduate colleges and universities from 1957 to 1967. This ten year period was a time of abundance and apathy compared with the years since. Rumblings at Berkeley in 1964 and subsequent scattered disruptions elsewhere sent out early warnings, but it was not until 1966 and 1967 that widespread storms racked institutions across the country. Harvard, for example, was struck during the 1967–1968 academic year. Three fundamental changes were already gathering momentum during the period studied by Dressel and DeLisle—new approaches to grading and evaluation were being explored, individualized programs that recognized differences in student backgrounds, preparation, and interests were expanding, and credit by examination and off-campus experiences were becoming more frequently recognized as legitimate parts of academic programs.

The educational system, high schools and colleges alike, has long required many bright students to chew the same food twice or thrice. Many high school seniors have had courses in mathematics, science, history, English, foreign languages, equal—not only in difficulty, but often in content—to those offered to college freshmen and sophomores. Advanced placement testing and credit by examination allow such students to bypass this distasteful, forced, refeeding, and to move on to a more stimulating and nutritious diet. In so doing, such practices make an important contribution, not only to efficient and productive use of time and energy, but also to students' continued interest in learning and self-development. Moreover, when granting credit helps students to get quickly through an institution and an existence which has little to offer them, it makes another important contribution.

These practices, however, are mixed blessings. There are negative potentials which must be dealt with if they are to become widely used. The tests focus attention on, and give priority to, a limited purpose of higher education, a questionable justification for its existence, and a narrow definition of successful achievement. Advanced placement tests, in most areas, assess a student's store of information and that's about all. In some areas like mathematics and to some extent the natural sciences, successful achievement also may require special skills or competence. However, advanced placement testing and credit by examination do not soundly assess the more complex intellectual skills of application, analysis, synthesis, and evaluation, all of which colleges aim to foster, and all of which make a difference in effective performance and effective living. Tests that assess learning of this kind for college students and show whether he has, or has not, grown in these areas, are not yet on the market—nor are they about to be.

Even if more complex tests were available, a larger problem would remain because many persons think that college should foster more than intellectual competence. Interpersonal competence is the chief requirement for job effectiveness, marriage and family living, social relationships, effective citizenship. Many persons think that higher education should help students broaden their horizons, expand their interests, become more aware of the complexities of life, clarify their purposes. There is also the belief that colleges should help students achieve autonomy and integrity sufficient to pursue their own existence and their own continued development. Advanced placement tests and credit by examination tell the student that all these dimensions of development, all these larger purposes, can be ignored, if he has enough information or special skills to pass the tests.

The negative consequences of advanced placement and credit by examination need not necessarily occur. These practices can be adopted and their benefits obtained, but other dimensions of learning and development valued by the institution should be clearly articulated. High schools and colleges should help students recognize that such development may be fostered or hampered by thoughtful decisions about their educational purposes and about their uses of the college or university. Having called attention to the diverse purposes to be pursued, colleges must then establish indices of performance which help students assess their own progress toward increased interpersonal competence, increased social awareness and complexity of outlook, increased autonomy and integrity. If such areas of development are explicitly recognized, advanced placement and progress through college will depend on more than the acquisition of skills and information. Learning and development will become individualized and integrated with other areas of major importance. Colleges and universities will offer a balanced program suitable to the current needs of individuals and society.

Even with such changes, another problem remains. Credit by examination moves out of the educational system most quickly those students who have the furthest to go. The brightest college freshmen usually can pass the tests, yet are furthest from their full potential. But their time in college is cut short. Farm production would drop dramatically with such a practice. Corn that grows to six feet and yields eight ears would be harvested early; corn that grows to four feet and yields fewer ears would be cultivated longer. Students aren't corn, and the metaphor may be corny, but the point is important. Educationally useful experiences should not be arbitrarily foreshortened. If colleges and universities cannot effectively educate bright students, then simply passing them on through and out of the system is hardly an effective response for the institutions or a sound solution for the students. For the brightest students who pursue education beyond high school, such acceleration means not only less time, but fewer options.

Honors programs, independent study, and tutorials all more than doubled in frequency between 1957 and 1967. Each of these permits students to work on topics closely tailored to their own interests and purposes at their own levels of competence and efficiency. But such programs vary greatly from campus to campus. On one campus independent study means plowing through a workbook, a series of prescribed readings, problems, exercises, and other activities, carefully designed to take the student where the teacher wants him to go and to make sure he covers the ground. The student may work on these materials alone, and may not attend class, but that is about all that is done independently. In other programs, usually in consultation with a teacher, one or more students set their own objectives, identify their own resources, lay out their own schedule of work, and indicate the products and criteria by which they will be judged. Tutorials and honors programs may similarily differ in the extent to which students or teachers define the objectives, content, structure, learning activities, and evaluational procedures. Some programs also require or assume that students work singly; other programs provide for joint efforts or coordinated activities where two or more students can work together and benefit from the exchange, stimulation, and amplified resources. All these programs, however implemented, expand the alternatives available to students and contribute to individualization.

Increased use of seminars, comprehensive examinations, and senior theses or projects not only enables increased flexibility for individuals, but also requires greater student use of the complex skills of interpretation, analysis, synthesis, application, and evaluation. When a student brings a report for scrutiny by peers and faculty, both reporter and critic gain; when ideas and information are shared in open but disciplined exchange, experience is enlarged and reconstructed; when information is drawn from diverse sources and applied to a complex question or a comprehensive project, working knowledge and intellectual skills are augmented.

In the past the educational changes have occurred primarily at elite institutions—and often have been provided only for the brightest and most advanced students even there. Consistent with historical traditions, which amplify opportunities for the rich and deny the poor, individualized programs have been made available to the students who need them least, who already have learned how to learn, who already have developed quite well the verbal abilities and intellectual skills required. Students who could most profit from such undertakings have seldom been given the chance to pursue them and to realize the gains that might come from the struggle. But that orientation is changing as individualized programs spread to less selective institutions, and as projects, seminars and comprehensive examinations become open to freshmen and sophomores as well as juniors and seniors.

This trend toward student self-definition of study areas and learning activities and toward diverse criteria and indices of performance can lead to effective learning, especially if the current anything-goes approach which characterizes many programs shifts toward greater emphasis on clear planning and sound evaluation. There is not much gain in trading tight prescription and rigid control for laissez-faire conditions, in trading irrelevant studies required by teachers for inconsequential studies based on student whimsy, in trading arbitrary standards for no standards at all. Reimposing teacher definitions and teacher standards on independent studies and on other activities to individualize instruction is no remedy. Instead of one totalism or another, an approach something like this is required (Dewey, 1938):

> To take advantage of the student's interest, to
> utilize it, is not a thing which is in any way opposed to

scholarship; it is just the reverse. No one teaching even
little children can have too much knowledge in order to
take best advantage of the child's interest. . . . Instead
of being treated as instrumental, if one does not have a
definitive knowledge of the subject matter under consideration, the whole thing will be inevitably diluted,
reduced, degraded to the level of the child's superficial
manifestations of interest. The mere interests which the
child has are of a more or less specific, transitory kind, in
stones, trees, and animals. It is a thing which cannot go
adequately utilized excepting by someone who has a very
thorough-going and specialized training in these matters.
The child's interest may be met without such a knowledge, but in that case there is no probability of any per-
manent growth of the thing, leading beyond itself and
amounting to anything. . . . The so-called new education, in realizing the value of interest has not sufficiently
realized the need of advanced and thorough and specialized scholarship, in order that the interest may be really
effective in the educational progress.

It is not, after all, so necessary that the individual
should follow this or that or the other particular subject
matter, as it is that he should have the liberty and opportunity to approach any and every subject matter in such
a way as to make his own special personality valid, to get
something out of all the subject matters from his own
point of view. . . . Genuine individuality . . . is con-
served so far as he is given the opportunity to approach
the subject matter, which objectively speaking is one and
the same for the whole class, from the point of view of his
own particular experiences and interests. Now in thus
approaching it, it does not mean that the subject matter
is entirely subordinated to his individuality, but simply
that there shall be some reciprocity, interaction, in order
that there may be a real transformation of the subject
matter in such a way as to effect a reconstruction in making over the experience of each individual.

John Dewey spoke those words in the 1890s. But if he were
alive today, he would most certainly pale to see such mismanagement

of interest-centered and experience-centered education. Unfortunately, just as some "progressive" teachers and schools during the
1930s overlooked Dewey's concern for teacher scholarship and
breadth of knowledge and for reciprocity and interaction, so have
many teachers and colleges of the 1970s. For Dewey, an effective
teacher took students' interests, concerns, and aspirations as a point
of departure, using their motive power to increase intellectual skills,
working knowledge, complexity of insight, and ultimately to generate
a yet larger range of purposes and interests to motivate further
learning. That is still the teacher's fundamental task, and it requires
thorough knowledge of pertinent concepts and information and
skillful use of resources. Audio-visual aids, computer-assisted instruction, direct experiences, all can play a part, but effective orchestration
is still required, and that is the responsibility of the teacher. If he
dodges it, he defaults.

Programs designed to connect living and learning and to use
off-campus experiences increased even more dramatically than the
various developments for individualizing teaching and learning. The
sharp increases in efforts to connect learning with living and to make
use of direct experiences on and off campus are an extension of the
other movements toward individualized programs. These programs
make it clear that direct experiences powerfully supplement the
verbal and numerical symbols found in print and pictures.

Until relatively recently print has reigned unchallenged, except for occasional laboratory exercises in the natural sciences and
rock hunting in geology. Television, film, tape recordings, and com-
puters are recent upstarts, but higher education is still hooked on
books. Encounters with print far outweight all others for credit. Yet
most things are learned more fully, more efficiently, and more
permanently otherwise. When the Bible says that Adam knew Eve,
it reminds us that *knowing* originally meant much more than the
pallid, abstract, and symbolic experience of words. Knowing requires
linking direct experiences to symbolic representations—words, pictures, numbers, rhythms, melodies—which we can carry with us
through time and space. Unless events are tied to symbolic posts,
they contribute little to education; symbols which have no counterparts in direct or vicarious experiences have only hazy and abstract
meanings. Verbalizing an experience can expand its meaning, reveal

subtleties and implications, suggest relationships with other experiences. But verbalization in the absence of relevant experience is empty. It has a hollow ring. One good poke, and the speaker collapses with a rush of hot air.

Unfortunately, as with independent study, laissez-faire attitudes and off-hand implementation often leave the educational values of study abroad, field work experience, community service, and nonresident terms largely unexploited. Few programs invest much time or energy helping students think through purposes, plans, and potential benefits in advance; few programs ask students to step aside and examine the experiences they are having; few programs require much contemplation afterward. Yet serious conversation and pertinent reading, writing, and reflection—before, during, and after such direct experiences—can increase awareness, enlarge perspective, and reinforce or temper outcomes.

These changes providing diverse programs, which take into account the varied backgrounds and purposes of the students served and make room for direct experiences and action programs on and off campus, challenge conceptual and institutional boundaries heretofore unquestioned. They were the beginnings, during the sixties, of two fundamental changes that go beyond simple rearrangement of subject matter and simple redistribution of credits and requirements.

First, higher education began to recognize that the impact of an educational program depends heavily on the characteristics of the students coming to it; that programs must be modified in response to changing student characteristics; that curricular requirements, teaching practices, instructional materials, and the study activities of students must be varied and flexible. Second, higher education recognized that there is much more to learn than what is in books and more to learning than listening to lectures.

Several new nontraditional institutions—Empire State College, University Without Walls, Community College of Vermont, Minnesota Metropolitan State College, New College at the University of Alabama, among others—are developing integrated programs aimed at recognizing individual differences and toward generating the wide array of resources for academic study and direct experiences needed for effective response to those differences.

The orientation shared by these new institutions is not to be

confused with that of the British Open University, a major innovation for that country. The approach of the British Open University
emphasizes very different assumptions. As Summerskill has observed,
"the heart of this program, no matter what is said about the weekly
television broadcasts, which are part of it, or the weekly radio
broadcasts, is still the Gutenberg innovation" (1972). Top notch
professors and instructors created a series of courses and an array of
high quality texts, tests, television and radio programs that carry the
instruction directly to the students through the mails and over the
air. Each student receives materials according to a regularized mail-
ing schedule, works his way through them, and sends in his completed
exercises for evaluation by an instructor or by a computer.

Much of the content is new or arranged in different form,
but the basic assumptions which underlie the program are not.
Although the program was developed for the working class people of
Great Britain, each of these diverse persons is expected to work his
way through the same subject matter, with identical materials, in
the same sequence, at about the same rate, and each takes the same
test scored against standard criteria. The criteria for evaluation are
held constant.

A few quotations from the Open University *Prospectus for
1972* illustrate the basic stance. Lord Crowther, Chancellor, in his
inaugural address said, "It has been said that there are two aspects
of education, both necessary. One regards the individual human
mind as a vessel of varying capacity, into which is to be poured as
much as it will hold of the knowledge and experience by which
society lives and moves. This is the Martha of education and we
shall have plenty of these tasks to perform. But the Mary regards the
human mind more as fire that has to be set alight and blown with
the divine efflatus. That we also take as our ambition." Note that
whether the student is a vessel to be filled or a lamp to be lighted,
the basic assumption is that he is *done to,* not *does.*

The course description for The Man Made World is illustrative. "Today the effect of the technology on society is greater than
ever before and not all of it is beneficial . . . The aim of the
course, therefore, is not only *to explain and demonstrate* the many
aspects of the way engineers, designers and others do their job, but
also to *assess* its impact upon us all." For science, the course descrip-

tion says, "The main aims of this course are *to present and explain* some of the concepts and principles of importance in modern science and *to show* how science, technology and society are interrelated." Credit in foundations courses "is awarded on the basis of assignments done during the course and an examination at the end of the course. The final examination consists of a written paper of up to three hours' length."

My purpose here is not to pass judgment on the soundness of the British Open University approach or on its appropriateness for the educational needs and resources of Great Britain at this time. My purpose is simply to make clear the difference between their orientation and assumptions and those of the new non-traditional institutions underway in the United States. In operational terms perhaps the difference is most sharply illustrated by constrasting the heart of the British Open University, its courses and course materials, with the heart of the nontraditional institutions, the individually designed program of study.

Empire State College calls this a "Contract" and its first Bulletin described it thus:

> The Contract which emerges from orientation and planning is an agreement between student and Mentor to a series of activities and responsibilities which both agree have merit and value. This Contract not only specifies the activities and responsibilities of the student—it does the same for the Mentor. It must, therefore, be drawn to take account of the realities which characterize both parties. The areas of competence and readiness must be appraised for the Mentor just as for the student. The work obligations, family responsibilities, availability, and energy of each must be recognized. Thus the Contract not only indicates what the student will be doing, where he will be doing it, with whom, and for how long, but also it indicates how often he will communicate with the Mentor, when, where, and for what purposes. Contracts will be reviewed by faculty members associated with the appropriate learning center and the coordinating center at Saratoga.
>
> By now it is clear that each student's Contract will

be his own, in some ways different from all other students, and in other ways similar. It also should be clear that a Contract can marshal diverse resources for learning by calling both on those persons provided by the Center and by the surrounding community.

The time dimension also is flexible. A student may work half time or full time, and his Contract for study may cover a month, a quarter, or a year. . . . Usually a reasonably short period . . . is preferable. . . . Unanticipated circumstances may arise. More often, the learning activities themselves lead to changing interests and emphases, and it is well to be able to accommodate these without major distortions of contracts or prior understandings. Indeed, one of the major outcomes of effective learning will be shifting priorities and expanding purposes. Contracts should recognize this and the time dimension is especially important.

The Contract is completed with an Evaluation Conference which includes the Mentor and others who were built into the evaluation plan. Such evaluation activities always turn an eye toward the future, so program planning for the next Contract has its seeds in this final meeting (1971, pp. 36, 37).

These new approaches which try to take clear account of individual differences and to build educational programs accordingly, also emphasize the importance of human contact. They recognize that the most powerful agents for individual learning and development are other individuals. Therefore they try to open up the range of diverse kinds of persons with whom a student can work and study and to provide resources that make those relationships possible.

But the emphasis on human contact does not mean that the wide ranging alternatives becoming available through advances in educational technology and programed learning are ignored. The potential of those developments has been recognized for some time, but remains largely unrealized. In the decade of the seventies, however, it is clear that the response of higher education to the increasing diversity of educational needs reflected by the wide range of new students, will include major developments in the new technologies for making complex concepts and information accessible to students. It is already clear that these new developments share two fundamental characteristics with the nontraditional institutions described above. First, the student will be an active agent, defining the pace, the content, and the complexity of the materials with which he works. Second, the varied learning systems will be responsive to a wide range of individual differences.

The impact of the new technologies is now becoming increasingly apparent and even large state universities are showing changes in faculty roles, in organization, and in concepts of teaching. Wayne Holtzman (personal communication) describes what is happening at the University of Texas:

> Computers are now used significantly for instructional purposes in forty-eight out of fifty-nine departments throughout the University. With support from the National Science Foundation a major program of computer-based education is now underway. In some areas the computer terminal is the primary tool for problem-solving, simulation, and instruction while in other fields it is only an occasional accessory. Through a network of exchange and special services, a large number of faculty and students are using computers for the first time. Chemistry 302, a second-semester course for majors, has been reorganized with one hour of lecture, one hour of small group discussion, and one hour of computer-based interactive programs each week. Individualized instruction by computer ranges from simulated laboratory experiments to drill and tutorial materials. As compared to a control group of Chemistry 302 students, those in the computer-assisted class covered more material and obtained higher grades on uniform departmental examinations.
>
> Another flexible option growing rapidly at the University of Texas involves Keller's Personalized System of Instruction (1968). A given course is broken down into small units or modules each containing explicit objectives, reading assignments, study questions, references and, where appropriate, a combination of computer-

based tutorials, audio-tapes, television, and self-assessment examinations. The student moves through the course at his own pace, demonstrating mastery of one unit before proceeding to the next. Proctors are always available for repeated testing and tutoring, providing a good deal of personal-social interaction. The Keller Plan has caught on particularly well in the College of Engineering where it is now used for a number of courses. Similar self-paced, individualized courses are available in chemistry, psychology, and education. Keller's Personalized System of Instruction provides a flexible framework within which the new technologies can be easily placed. The student becomes more responsible for his own learning at a time, place, and rate that fits his personal style and his other objectives.

Use of the new technologies in self-paced tutorial programs is particularly attractive as a way of taking into account individual differences among learners. Students are distributed according to the rate at which they learn rather than how well or poorly they have mastered a skill or subject matter in a fixed period of time. This feature is especially important for the student who has been poorly prepared for college by his past academic failures. Successful completion of small units of learning produces a sense of accomplishment which may even lead a student into liking a subject and wanting more of it. At the same time, frequent assessment and branching are essential so that capable students may move through the curriculum as efficiently as possible.

Some persons see a major conflict between the new nontraditional approaches exemplified by institutions like the University Without Walls or Empire State College and the rapidly burgeoning developments in educational technology and programed learning materials. The possibility of conflict is certainly there if the new institutions ignore or are irrational about the contributions to individual learning which are made by systematically organized materials which students can use to learn on their own. And the conflict is there if organized programs, whether computer managed or in print, do not take account of individual differences and are not sufficiently flexible so that diverse individuals can tailor them to their own backgrounds and cognitive styles. In my own judgment, however, this conflict is neither necessary nor likely. Instead I see the development of two approaches that are powerfully complementary.

On the one hand a new kind of educational institution is getting underway oriented toward individual students. It is organized so as to recognize their different strengths and weaknesses and their different interests and aspirations. It is developing the human resources and the competence to help these individuals make sound plans for their own learning and to help them make sound judgments about the kinds of resources they can best use to achieve the knowledge, competence, and personal development they value. Educational technology and varied approaches toward the development of systematically organized programs will dramatically expand the range of resources on which these students can draw.

On the other hand these new institutions, with their emphasis on individualized learning, provide ideal testing grounds for the new fruits of educational technology and programed learning. These developments will make many more tools and instrumentalities available and by doing so will increase the possibilities for effective education for each of the diverse individuals served by these and by other two and four year colleges and universities during the seventies.

# 4

# Persons and
# Principles

*T*he general findings presented in forthcoming chapters, and the statistics on which they rest, present a powerful picture of the general differences among those who commute and those who reside at colleges and universities—in entering characteristics, in college experiences, and in educational outcomes. But it is important to remember that there are individual persons behind the generalizations, that the statistics are only crude and highly depersonalized summations of vital processes and dynamic struggles of a diverse array of human beings. Like the figures that predict and report infant mortality rates, holiday automobile fatalities, the numbers of civilians or soldiers killed and wounded in Southeast Asia, the statistics do not communicate the powerful physical, psychological, and emotional load that each digit represents.

To my knowledge there are no detailed longitudinal case studies of commuting students as they proceed through college. But one report which makes a substantial beginning is Schuchman's *Double Life of the Commuter College Student* (1966) and many of my comments draw heavily on the substance of that article.

Joe Residential begins to leave home when he chooses a

residential college. His departure gathers momentum as he scans Esquire for fashion forecasts, decides what to pack, and shops for clothes and other accouterments necessary for effective self-presentation at Ivy Private. His father and mother are anxious and full of advice; he is anxious himself. Finally, his parents escort him to the train, plane, or dormitory, bid brave farewells, and go home. Their departure marks a new status for Joe; it unequivocally begins a new chapter in his existential book. And it begins a new chapter for his parents. The family will never be the same again.

After initial uncertainties and anxieties Joe finds that college is not as difficult or as different as he expected. Many other freshmen share his attitudes and aspirations, and he finds friends who come from similar families, communities, and high schools. The academic challenges, if they exist, are not as overwhelming as he feared. He does meet pressures to make certain changes in style, behavior, attitudes, and values. Through lengthy bull sessions with classmates reaching to resolve their own uncertainties and conflicts and through behavioral experimentation, he begins to clarify his positions and beliefs.

When Joe goes home for Christmas he has become an individual quite separate from his family. He sees them and his relationships with them differently, and they see a difference in him. They treat him with greater respect, grant him greater freedom, listen more thoughtfully to what he says. They may also dislike some of his new styles and disagree with some of his new values and attitudes. Vacation, therefore, includes not only the comforts of home but also the conflicts of generations, even though Joe's upper-middle-class parents share many of his views and had similar experiences during their college careers. Both Joe and his parents are often somewhat relieved as the vacation draws to a close and he can return to the college environs where he now feels more at home.

It is different for the commuters, Chauncy and Charlie, who go to "concrete public." They may have shopped for clothes, but they did not pack. On opening day they jump in the car or climb on the bus, plod through registration, and go back home. Their parents ask what they are going to take, whom they met, and how it was— and keep on asking throughout the semester and the year. If their parents have fussed about health, grades, social contacts, recreational activities, bedtime, they continue to fuss. They continue to expect to know what Charlie or Chauncy is doing, when, and with whom, how much money he has and how he intends to spend it, what he plans to do tomorrow and next week. If Chauncy and Charlie have had chores around the house, they continue most of them. If they have been working, job arrangements may be modified but they often continue. If they have received a monthly allowance, it may be increased, but the practice stands.

For Chauncy and Charlie no landmark signals a new existence over the horizon, no rite-of-passage marks a new status, no increased geographical, temporal, or psychological distance creates a space for significant redefinition of relationships. The prophet remains in his own country.

Chauncy and Charlie come from quite different family and cultural backgrounds. Chauncy goes to college to maintain and augment the family's social and economic status. His parents are college graduates or have had some college experience, and their economic status has been sufficient to provide him with a reasonable array of enriching experiences and material benefits. He is propelled into college because this is what his parents have always intended and what he has always expected. But once in college he wonders whether he really wants to be there, whether he really wants to be the doctor, lawyer, or Indian chief that his father is or would have him become. He may feel that his parents' life and future has been loaded onto his shoulders; the success of their lives, and their investments in him, rests on his success. He owes them everything. How can he deny their expectations? How can he take time to explore new interests? How can he take a summer to goof off, to bum around the countryside or to go overseas?

The pressures of parental expectation, indebtedness, and financial dependency that operate for Chauncy also operate for many residential students. Studies of Yale dropouts by Keniston and Hirsch (1970), and of dropouts from other residential institutions in the northeast by Levenson and Kohn (1964) and others, document the same dynamics at work. But Chauncy's difficulties are compounded by his continual contact with his parents and by their persistent scrutiny and constant benevolent concern. His problems are further compounded by the difficulties he encounters in establishing significant relationships with other students and with faculty members and other adults, who are part of the college community and life style he wants to join or, at least, to explore and test.

Charlie's background is quite different. His folks often belong to the working class and to religious or ethnic minorities. They often are oriented more toward past traditions or sheer survival in the present than toward future conditions or long-range visions. They are attached to familiar ways and surroundings. They seek and hold jobs that offer structure and security. They are sacrificing to send Charlie to college and are not entirely convinced it is the right thing to do. They have not gone to college and some of them have not completed high school.

Charlie's father brings home his weekly wages earned by the hour on a construction job, in a factory, driving a truck or bus, or in some one of the other thousands of routine jobs that produce the goods and services on which the rising standard of living in the United States depends. He belongs to the American Legion or VFW. He bowls one night a week in one of the leagues that fill the alleys during the winter, and when he goes to the neighborhood tavern to heist a few with the boys he does not take his wife.

Charlie usually has been working to carry some of his own own expenses and to help the family. He should be courteous, obedient, thrifty, neat, and respectful, especially in front of his parents and toward other adults. These expectations do not change simply because Charlie is now taking his courses in college instead of high school.

But despite the fact that college may be only a streetcar ride away, when Charlie gets there he often steps into an unfamiliar world, full of persons different from those he has known in the past, with ideas, attitudes, values, and life styles he has not experienced directly before or had to think about seriously. There are books and magazines that never were around his house, there are open discussions of issues that never were mentioned at his supper table, and many that were never even considered. He knows that his parents would be antagonized if they came to know some of these persons, books, and ideas.

When he goes home he returns to a family where the forces that have maintained the family equilibrium and stability are still powerfully at work. Each new attitude, aspiration, or style of life that Charlie brings home threatens that equilibrium and may cause overt conflict, covert hostility, or indirect resistance. Home becomes less comfortable, conflict is not limited to vacations, there is no haven at college.

Charlie, therefore, must not only cope with academic challenges for which he is not well prepared, and with the personal questions raised by new life styles and future possibilities, but also with family constraints, misunderstandings, and misgivings. He is caught between two cultures where identification with one often requires denial, or at least neglect, of the other. But usually he still must depend on the old for financial and emotional support while he aspires toward the new for future economic gains and personal expansion.

Under these conditions Charlie may become immobilized at the intersection where the attractions of the new are balanced by the pains of disengagement from the old. When this happens his problems may be compounded by increasing feelings similar to those that afflict Chauncy as he is caught between his parents' aspirations and pressures and his own divergent interests and concerns. Apathy and disinterest set in. It is hard to concentrate on school work, to keep up with assignments, to find challenge in new ideas and experiences, and to take satisfaction from difficult tasks successfully completed. Going to classes, studying for exams, preparing papers, increasingly require major acts of will and become increasingly meaningless activities. In time, even relationships with friends and favorite recreational activities may lose their appeal, and life becomes a stale business of going through the motions.

There are two ways out. One is to drop out of college and go back to work. Often this return to work may be temporary. Either Charlie's parents, Charlie himself, or both, as they experience more fully the limited employment alternatives and contemplate more unequivocally the restricted range of possibilities for advancement and increased income, recognize more forcefully the value of a college degree. The parents become more willing to accept the other problematic elements that seem to go along with it; Charlie is more willing and ready to bear their concerns or to simply ignore them in the recognition that neither he nor they can do anything about them.

The other way out is to focus more sharply on a clearly defined vocational objective where concrete progress is observable and where the rewards in terms of income, material possessions and increased status are explicit and apparent. This sharpened focus leaves other more complex dimensions of development to shift for themselves. It sets aside until a later day the plaguing questions of attitudes and values, of autonomy and social responsibility. Broad issues of identity and purpose collapse around an occupational definition that provides a respectable answer even though, as the research of Beardslee and O'Dowd (1962) demonstrated, most students can say very little about how the actual hours and days are spent in the occupations for which they are preparing.

As we go beyond the individual lives of commuters and residents to data on groups, we see processes at work which are consistent with general research and theory concerning college impacts on student development. (See for example, Astin and Panos, 1969; Chickering, 1969; Feldman and Newcomb, 1969; Katz and Associates, 1968; Heath, 1968; Newcomb, Koenig, and others, 1967; Raushenbush, 1964; Sanford, 1966.)

(1) Peers, parents, faculty members, and reference groups and cultures they represent, are the principal developmental agents for college students. They provide support during periods of emotional stress. They amplify, dampen, and distort sounds and pressures from the establishment. They provide alternate sources of gratification, alternate behaviors and attitudes, alternate philosophies and life styles, and they can constrain and limit the range of new experiences and consequent changes.

(2) Individuals change as they encounter new conditions, experiences, and new kinds of persons for which preestablished responses are not adequate, for which new skills, new behaviors, new words, concepts, and attitudes are required.

(3) The range of significant encounters with new conditions, experiences, and new persons is most restricted for high school graduates who continue to live at home after entering college. Many of their high school friendships continue as do many other activities and responsibilities they have been carrying. They go to class at the college and go home.

(4) Few commuters exercise choice in college selection.

They attend a nearby college, and if its dominant attitudes and values differ substantially from their own, they do not have many alternatives. They cannot easily travel far to find a better fitting institution.

Thus, it is not surprising that the data in later chapters show that students who live with their parents change less than the general college going population, and significantly less than those who leave home and move into dormitories. Students who live in private accommodations off-campus are mixed in this regard, as Chapters Six and Seven indicate. Some of them are local students who have moved out of their parents' house. Others have sought the privacy and freedom of living alone or with another close friend or acquaintance. Still others are required to live off-campus because college housing was not available and have teamed up with others as best they can to find housing and to manage it together. (Most married freshmen, for example, are in this category.) Because they are so diverse, canceling forces obscure and confuse the general findings for these off-campus students as a whole.

However, because these students who live in off-campus private accommodations have themselves chosen their roommates, apartmentmates, or housemates, the range of different kinds of persons they come to know and must learn to live with is more restricted than is the case for dormitory residents who usually are thrown together with others from the full range admitted by the institution. Moreover, like their peers who live at home, these students have less time for extracurricular activities; although they do not travel so far to the campus, often they have to cope with food and housekeeping chores.

The subsequent information about these students in off-campus accommodations not only suggests their intermediate position between dormitory students and those living at home in terms of the range of new conditions, experiences, persons they encounter, but also reflects the diverse characteristics within this general population. To understand well the consequences of such living arrangements requires more precise analyses of the major subgroups within it. But despite these differences, the findings for this mixed group tend to support the basic theoretical notions outlined above.

In sum, according to theory, dormitory residents because

of their distance from home, new persons they must live with, immediate presence on  campus, and their ready access to varied campus activities have much more frequent and more intense exposure to experiences which challenge preexisting competence, behaviors, and attitudes; and to cope with these challenges they change. This pattern should differ for nondormitory groups; the difference should be most clearly found when students living at home are compared with college residents.

The empirical evidence in the following chapters is clear. Residents, in response to immersion in a college environment, change most during the first two years. They decelerate and may even slightly regress after that, as they move back toward the home culture as graduation approaches. They change most quickly in the nonintellectual areas where the differences between high school and college are greatest. And change in intellectual areas accelerates as college courses and patterns of study become more challenging. In contrast, commuters' change is slower. They are constrained by internal conflicts and by pressures from parents, peers, and prior community. These constraints operate with least force for intellectual development, where the college experiences of commuters and residents are most similar. Thus the commuters more quickly approximate the scores of residents in the intellectual area. But because substantial differences exist, and persist, in the range of noncourse experiences and interpersonal relationships, nonintellectual changes occur more slowly. Beginning college with fewer advantages than resident students, commuters as a group slip further and further behind residents despite these changes. And, as a consequence, college has the effect of widening the gap between the have-not students and the haves.

# 5

# *Student Characteristics*

$P$rior research concerning differences between commuters and residents has revealed that place of residence during college varies according to socioeconomic background, with fraternity students typically from the highest status families, followed by students in dormitories, then by those in rooming houses, and finally by those living at home. Compared with residents, commuters more frequently report problems concerning interpersonal relationships with peers and family, and financial problems. Commuters, much more frequently than residents, see vocational preparation as the primary purpose of college, and they more frequently major in business administration or engineering. They obtained lower grades in high school, and they are less interested in national and world affairs.

The results of my studies with the American Council on Education (ACE) are consistent with these earlier findings. Two major analyses were undertaken: multiple regression analyses, which examined attitudes and behaviors of 5351 students selected randomly from 38,000 students who responded to a follow-up questionnaire at the end of their freshman year; and reanalysis of responses to a survey, of the next freshman class, which was completed by 169,190 freshmen entering 270 diverse two- and four-year colleges and universities. Weighting procedures applied to this sample generate the best currently available figures for the whole nation. Weighting procedures also permit analysis and normative statements for nine different types of institutions: public and private two-year colleges; public, private nonsectarian, Protestant, and Catholic four-year colleges; technological institutions; public and private universities. Table 1 gives further information about the institutions and the student samples. (For detailed discussion of sampling methods and weighting procedures and for tables relating to these methods and procedures, see "National Norms for Entering College Freshmen—Fall 1969," 1969).

The survey results and multiple regression analyses revealed differences in parental background and finances, high school achievements and experiences, college plans and future aspirations, anticipated college experiences and activities, and attitudes and beliefs. One difference to keep in mind throughout this discussion of student characteristics is that although most freshmen are eighteen years or older, 11 percent of the commuters are over twenty, compared with only 3 percent of the residents.

Residents more frequently grew up in the suburbs, whereas commuters grew up in moderate-size towns or cities or in large cities. These rough differences in living locations are crude expressions of parental, occupational, and educational backgrounds. Fifty-two percent of the residents estimate their parents' incomes above fifteen thousand dollars, and 13 percent above thirty-five thousand dollars, compared with only 21 percent and 4 percent, respectively, for the commuters. Residents' fathers are much more frequently businessmen, clergymen, secondary school educators, doctors, and lawyers, while commuters' fathers are more frequently skilled, semi-skilled, or unskilled workers. These occupational and income differences are strongly associated with educational differences. Thirty-one percent of the commuters' parents did not complete high school, compared with 20 percent for the residents; 36 percent of the residents' parents have a college degree or higher, compared with 19 percent for the commuters. These differences in parental education, occupation, and income are such that residents are more often

## Table 1.

### NUMBER OF INSTITUTIONS AND STUDENTS USED IN COMPUTING WEIGHTED NATIONAL NORMS FOR 1969

| | | Number of Entering Freshmen[a] | | |
| | | | Weighted Totals | |
| Norm Group | Number of Institutions | Actual Participants | Number | Men, Percent |
|---|---|---|---|---|
| All institutions | 270 | 169,190 | 1,637,831 | 56.6 |
| All 2-year colleges | 46 | 23,520 | 584,942 | 61.2 |
| All 4-year colleges | 183 | 69,237 | 598,585 | 51.6 |
| All universities | 41 | 76,433 | 454,304 | 57.4 |
| 2-year public colleges | 25 | 17,234 | 436,997 | 61.9 |
| 2-year private colleges | 21 | 6,286 | 147,945 | 59.0 |
| Technological institutions | 11 | 6,337 | 44,764 | 98.6 |
| 4-year public colleges[b] | 21 | 18,328 | 304,631 | 46.3 |
| 4-year private non-sectarian colleges[b] | 66 | 21,811 | 107,708 | 47.2 |
| 4-year Protestant colleges[b] | 48 | 14,502 | 92,701 | 51.6 |
| 4-year Catholic colleges[b] | 37 | 8,259 | 48,781 | 51.2 |
| Public universities | 26 | 59,534 | 365,069 | 56.5 |
| Private universities | 15 | 16,899 | 89,235 | 61.1 |
| Nonsectarian colleges for men | 12 | 4,042 | 10,923 | — |
| Nonsectarian colleges for women | 14 | 4,638 | 20,488 | — |
| Nonsectarian coed colleges | 40 | 13,131 | 76,297 | 52.6 |
| Catholic colleges for men | 7 | 1,780 | 10,562 | — |
| Catholic colleges for women | 15 | 2,301 | 12,121 | — |
| Catholic coed colleges | 15 | 4,178 | 26,098 | 56.1 |
| Predominantly Negro colleges | 11 | 3,668 | 39,465 | 47.0 |

[a] First time, full-time.
[b] Includes only liberal arts and teachers' colleges.

supported by parental and family financial aid, whereas commuters more often must rely on savings or employment income.

The differences in parental background are associated with significant differences in high school achievements, experiences, and activities. Proportionally, half as many commuters (9 percent) as residents (18 percent) graduated from high school with grade point averages of A−, A, or A+. Substantially more commuters had averages of C+ C, or D (37 percent for commuters versus 25 percent for residents). Consequently, more residents ranked among the top 10 percent in their high school class and fewer were in the bottom half, and more than twice as many residents as commuters won National Merit Scholarships.

The differences in high school achievements become even more pronounced in extracurricular activities. On a list of twelve items, residents are substantially higher on all but one—"won a prize or an award in an art competition"—where there is a slight difference in favor of the commuters. The differences are greatest for "was elected president of one or more student organizations," "won a varsity letter in sports," "edited the school paper, yearbook, or literary magazine," "had poems, stories, essays, or articles published," "had a major part in a play," and "was a member of a scholastic honor society."

These differences in achievements are accompanied by similarly consistent differences in high school experiences and activities. On thirty-two of thirty-four different items, residents outnumber commuters. The following items, listed in order of magnitude, reflect the greatest differences: "tutored another student," "checked out a library book," "read poetry not assigned in a course," "discussed politics," "voted in a student election," "discussed religion," "discussed sports," "played a musical instrument," "asked a teacher for advice," "visited an art gallery," "worked on a local, state, or national political campaign," "arranged a date for another student," "discussed my future with my parents."

Substantially more commuters than residents had applied only to the college they were attending (61 percent versus 38 percent). Residents, in contrast, much more frequently had applied to at least two other colleges (41 percent versus 20 percent).

Residents more frequently than commuters judge several

items "essential" or "very important" to their future lives. In order of magnitude they are: "keep up with political affairs," "become a community leader," "develop a philosophy of life," "have friends different from me," and "influence social values."

These differences in long-range objectives are accompanied by differences in degree plans. Proportionally, three times as many commuters as residents plan to stop with an associate degree (13 percent versus 4 percent), whereas substantially more residents plan to obtain at least a master's degree (57 percent versus 43 percent).

In comparison with commuters, residents more frequently predict they will join a fraternity or sorority, change their major field or their career choice, and marry within a year after college. Although the differences are quite small, residents also predict more frequently that they will protest against military policy, college administrative policy, and racial or ethnic policies.

Surprisingly perhaps, widespread differences in attitudes do not accompany these other differences. On a set of items concerning federal policies, commuters and residents differ on only two: nine out of ten students believe that the government should become more involved in pollution control, and residents outnumber commuters 92 percent to 89 percent; about 35 percent of the students think the government should become more involved in providing special benefits for veterans, and commuters outnumber residents 37 percent to 32 percent. Another set of items on diverse topics also reflects few differences in attitude. Residents more frequently agree that "college officials have the right to regulate student behavior off campus" and that "under some conditions abortions should be legalized"; commuters more often agree that "the chief benefit of college is that it increases one's earning power."

Basically then, on a national basis, when students are aggregated for all two- and four-year colleges and universities, the residents are the haves and the commuters, the have nots. Like any oversimplification, however, this distinction can be misleading if applied indiscriminately because there are significant variations among different types of institutions.

The university commuter has his own special combination of characteristics. Substantial differences occur between commuters and residents in parental occupation, income, and educational background, in high school achievements, experiences, and activities, and in long-range aspirations; but the two groups are similar in degree plans. This similarity is especially surprising in the private universities, where the differences in the other areas are most pronounced. Put most sharply, the commuting student in the private university, compared with his resident counterpart, combines high academic aspirations with limited resources and past achievements. Despite the fact that his parental background and high school achievement may often exceed those of his commuting peers who have chosen other institutions, the gap between where he starts and where he hopes to finish is great.

In the private colleges there are substantial differences between commuters and residents in parental background and in high school achievements and experiences. Although the commuters have "more" than their commuting counterparts in the public institutions, there is still a large gap in background and preparation between them and their residential competitors. Yet, despite this gap and despite some major differences in long-run goals, there is little difference in degree aspirations. Like their counterparts in the private universities, the commuters hope to achieve the same academic levels as do the residents, who enter with a strong head start.

These findings are of critical importance for private four-year colleges and universities. Educational practices in many of these institutions create competitive environments which commuters must enter with substantial handicaps in relation to the residents. The institutions set up a race on a mile track, but commuters start a quarter of a mile behind. The point of education, obviously, is to accelerate learning and development. Most important, therefore, is how far a person travels during the experience, not whether he reaches some arbitrarily defined finish abreast of his peers. Unfortunately, however, the evidence indicates that the gap between commuters and residents will continue to increase until private institutions develop programs which recognize the different starting points of many commuters.

The variations on the theme played by the public four-year colleges may be the most important to recognize because of the large numbers of students they serve. In these institutions parents' educational background, occupation, and income are similar for residents and commuters. But, contrary to the usual pattern, commuters have more liberal attitudes concerning federal policies and social issues, higher grade point averages in high school and more of the academic honors and recognition that accompany superior academic performance. Residents report more extracurricular achievements than do commuters.

However, the degree plans and long-run objectives of residents and commuters in public colleges are similar, closing a gap that is part of the distinction between them.

The Protestant and Catholic colleges offer another variation. The typical differences in parents' education, occupation, and income level appear, but in these institutions such differences are not accompanied by differences between commuters and residents in attitudes or in levels of religious commitment. Commuters have somewhat higher grades in high school, more frequently obtaining B or B+. These are the only institutions with no major differences in extracurricular activities and achievements. In these colleges, as in the public ones, college plans and future aspirations are similar for commuters and residents.

The pattern at the technological institutions is different. The distinction holds between parents' education, occupation, and income, as well as for academic and extracurricular achievements in high school. However, commuters more frequently hold liberal positions concerning federal policies and social issues, while residents are consistently more conservative. Yet when residents describe their long-range goals, they more frequently express social concern and commitment to making social contributions, while the long-range plans of the more liberal commuters more frequently involve occupational success, principally in engineering.

In the public and private two-year colleges the distinctions collapse rather sharply, with few major differences noted between commuters and residents. In a few areas the typical generalizations are reversed so that, for example, in both public and private colleges residents tend to have had lower high school grades, and in the public colleges the residents more frequently do not intend to continue beyond the associate degree. This collapsing of the differences probably occurs because entrants at both types of institutions, compared with their four-year counterparts, tend to be at a disadvantage on all the major areas tapped by the ACE freshmen survey. Therefore, there is not much room for them to differ from one another.

Differences in the entering characteristics of residents and commuters are worth examining in detail because of their implications for educational policies and practices. It is by now a truism that the consequences of particular educational programs depend in large measure upon the characteristics students bring to them. Residents and commuters, who differ substantially in background, encounter similar curricular requirements, similar standards and grading practices, similar cultural pressures and institutional expectations. Because of differences at entrance, outcomes are different—not only in college experiences and activities but also in patterns of learning and development. And the gap between the two groups becomes larger rather than smaller. These undesirable social and educational outcomes, which follow from the undiscriminating application of set requirements, must be dealt with by recognizing the differences between commuters and residents and by creating educational alternatives better suited to the characteristics of each. These variations and the consequent programs will depend heavily on the particular type of institution under consideration.

# 6

# College
# Experiences

*T*he studies reported in this chapter demonstrate that the high school differences in experiences, activities, and achievements continue through the college years. Residents engage more fully with the academic program and associated intellectual activities. They have more frequent and wider ranging contact with faculty members and fellow students. They more frequently participate in extracurricular activities and assume positions of leadership. They more frequently attend cultural events and discuss political, religious, and social issues.

Because learning and personal development in college is influenced by the experiences and activities students pursue while there, these differences between commuters and residents deserve careful scrutiny. The results unequivocally confirm personal observations, impressionistic reports, and the empirical findings from earlier studies. They leave no question that there is need for creative programs that will broaden the college experience for the commuting student. For if such programs are not developed, the gap between the commuter and the resident student, so evident among entering freshmen, will continue to grow rather than diminish during the college years.

Multiple regression analyses, undertaken principally to examine student change during the freshman year, produced some evidence concerning differences in experiences, activities, and future plans of residents and commuters. These analyses were carried out for a random sample of 5351 students selected from the 26,806 who completed both the initial freshman survey and the follow-up questionnaire at the end of their first year. The students in this sample were distributed among living locations such that 75.8 percent had lived in college dormitories, 22.4 percent at home with their parents, 3.7 percent in another private home, apartment, or room, and 1.2 percent in a fraternity or sorority.

The data contain no surprises. Residents are more frequently supported by parental aid and repayable loans. They are more frequently involved with fraternities and sororities and more often participate in intramural athletics and in various social activities—playing bridge, drinking beer, participating in demonstrations (Do you remember the girl who ran through the dorm asking, "What do you wear to a riot?"). The residents also more frequently discuss religion and politics and attend foreign movies. They are more frequently guests in a teacher's home. They plan to return to the same college and to be full time students more frequently than their commuting peers. Commuters more often finance their education through personal savings or employment. They also more frequently plan to major in business administration or engineering.

These analyses also generated findings for students living in other private homes, rooms, or apartments off campus. The experiences and activities of these students are more similar to the commuters living at home than to the dormitory residents.

More detailed findings came from analyses of the total group of 26,806 students, which produced separate scores for students living at home, in private off-campus housing, and in college dormitories. On every item regarding extracurricular activities—except rode on a motorcycle and got a traffic ticket—students who live at home with their parents score lower than students who live in dormitories. Students who live in other private housing score between the two groups on 4 items; they are highest on items concerning racial and Vietnam demonstrations and lowest on visits to an art gallery or museum.

Commuters who live at home consistently have least frequent exchange with teachers in or out of class, least frequently tutor or study with another student, and least frequently discuss religion or politics. Commuters who live in other private housing again tend to fall between the other two groups, except that they least frequently play tennis and study with other students.

Students who live in private off-campus housing are least satisfied with their college and least frequently plan to return for full-time study, and students who live at home fall between them and the residents.

It is difficult to know just what to make of data like these, which average responses for rather general options, for large numbers of students. The scores, almost by necessity, must vary around the midpoint of the alternatives offered, and the score differences among the three groups of students who were tested were not great. However, the internal consistency is such that these data do present really clear documentation of consistent differences in the freshman experiences of students who live at home with their parents and those who live in college dormitories. And they also suggest yet another constellation for those diverse kinds of students who live in private off-campus housing.

These same analyses were carried out separately for public and private universities, public, private nonsectarian, Protestant, Catholic four-year colleges, public and private two-year colleges, and technological institutions. In every one of these nine different types of institutions the same differences in the college experiences and activities of commuters who live at home and dormitory residents were found. These differences persist even though general score levels vary from one type of institution to another. For example, both commuters and residents participate in organized demonstrations more frequently in the private universities and in the public and private nonsectarian and Catholic four-year colleges, but scores for commuters are consistently lower. Similarly, students are more frequently guests in a teacher's home in the Protestant and Catholic colleges, and they more frequently discuss religion in the private nonsectarian colleges; and although commuter scores are higher than resident scores in other types of institutions, within each institution their scores are lower than residents.

These consistent differences between commuters and residents across different types of institutions are worth special attention for this reason. When the background characteristics of commuters and residents were compared, some types of institutions departed markedly from the general findings of data aggregated for all types of institutions. In the public four-year colleges and in the technological institutions, for example, the general relationships between commuters and residents are reversed in some areas, so that commuters tend to have better high school records or to hold more liberal sociopolitical attitudes. In the Protestant and Catholic colleges, for example, in several areas there are essentially no differences between commuters and residents. A good deal of research, carried out principally by Astin and his associates at the American Council on Education, has demonstrated that the outcomes of college depend heavily on the characteristics students bring with them at entrance. The findings from these studies of commuters and residents in different types of institutions, however, indicate that the differences in their college experiences remain consistent, despite the shifting patterns of relationships between the two groups when their entering characteristics are considered. Therefore, it seems clear that for these subgroups at least, major aspects of the college experience are independent of student characteristics at entrance.

Research and theory also suggest that institutional size and selectivity influence college experiences and student development. (See for example, Chickering, 1969, and various publications by Astin, principally Astin and Panos, 1968, 1969, 1970.) It seems useful, therefore, to analyze these data according to several combinations of size and selectivity.

Table 2 reports the selectivity levels used by the ACE Office of Research and the aptitude test scores for entering freshmen used as criteria for each level. Table 3 illustrates one outcome from this approach by listing twenty-seven highly selective institutions that usually appear at level eight. Virtually all the institutions for which no estimates were available have very low selectivity scores. The analyses reported here combined levels seven and eight, and combined level one with the "No Estimate Available" institutions. Small, medium and large institutions were sorted according to different selectivity levels to produce eleven subgroups shown in Table 4—four selectivity

## Table 2

SELECTIVITY LEVELS OF HIGHER EDUCATIONAL INSTITUTIONS, 1968
($N = 2,319$)

| College Selectivity Level | Corresponding Range of Student Mean Scores | | Institutions | |
|:---:|:---:|:---:|:---:|:---:|
| | SAT V + M | ACT Composite | Number | Percent |
| 8 | 1320 or higher | 30 or higher | 27 | 1.2 |
| 7 | 1236–1319 | 28–29 | 43 | 1.8 |
| 6 | 1154–1235 | 26–27 | 85 | 3.7 |
| 5 | 1075–1153 | 25–26 | 141 | 6.1 |
| 4 | 998–1074 | 23–24 | 342 | 14.7 |
| 3 | 926– 997 | 21–22 | 331 | 14.3 |
| 2 | 855– 925 | 19–20 | 273 | 11.8 |
| 1 | 854 or lower | 18 or lower | 281 | 12.1 |
| No Estimate Available | 854[a] | 18[a] | 796 | 34.3 |

[a] Estimate of the average test scores of students entering institutions in this category.

levels for small and medium size institutions, and three for large ones.

The results from these analyses are generally similar to those obtained when the varied types of two- and four-year colleges and universities were examined separately. Thus this additional study demonstrates consistent differences in commuter-resident experiences and activities despite major variations in institutional size and selectivity.

The results from these studies of experiences and activities during the freshman year are easily summarized. Students who lived at home with their parents participated in various kinds of cultural and extracurricular activities less frequently than dormitory residents, and their relationships with faculty members and fellow college students were more limited. Students who lived at home were less

*Table 3.*

TWENTY-SEVEN HIGHLY SELECTIVE INSTITUTIONS
RATED 8 IN COLLEGE SELECTIVITY LEVEL

| *Enrollment = 20,000 or more* | *Enrollment = 1,000-2,499* |
|---|---|
| Harvard University | Amherst College |
| *Enrollment = 10,000-19,999* | California Institute of Technology |
| Stanford University | Carleton College |
| University of Chicago | Pomona College |
| *Enrollment = 5,000-9,999* | Reed College |
| | Smith College |
| Brown University | Swarthmore College |
| Massachusetts Institute of Technology | Wellesley College |
| Yale University | Wesleyan University |
| | Williams College |
| *Enrollment = 2,500-4,999* | *Enrollment = 500-999* |
| Brandeis University | Bryn Mawr College |
| Dartmouth College | Haverford College |
| Princeton University | |
| Rice University | *Enrollment = 200-499* |
| University of California at San Diego | Harvey Mudd College |
| | New College |
| | *Enrollment less than 200* |
| | Deep Springs College |
| | Webb Institute of Naval Architecture |

satisfied with their college and less frequently planned to return or to study full-time. These differences occurred in both the public and private two-and four-year colleges, and in the public and private universities. And they occurred regardless of institutional size and selectivity.

The studies of experiences and activities using data for the total years at college consistently document the findings for the freshman year. They provide much more detailed evidence concerning the differences between commuters and residents in extracurricular participation and in relationships with fellow students

*Table 4.*

INSTITUTIONAL SUBGROUPS BASED ON SIZE AND SELECTIVITY

| | Average Entering Test Scores | |
| Type of Institution | SAT Total | ACT Composite |
|---|---|---|
| *Small Institutions* (Enrollments of 2,499 or less) | | |
| Non-selective | 925 or below | 20 or below |
| Low Selectivity | 926–1074 | 21–24 |
| Moderate Selectivity | 1075–1235 | 25–27 |
| Highly Selective | 1236 or above | 28 or above |
| *Medium Size Institutions* (Enrollments of 2,500–9,000) | | |
| Non-selective | 925 or below | 20 or below |
| Low Selectivity | 926–1074 | 21–24 |
| Moderate Selectivity | 1075–1235 | 25–27 |
| Highly Selective | 1236 or above | 28 or above |
| *Large Institutions* (Enrollments of 10,000 or more) | | |
| Low Selectivity | 1074 or below | 24 or below |
| Moderate Selectivity | 1075–1235 | 25–27 |
| Highly Selective | 1236 or above | 28 or above |

and faculty members. They also provide evidence concerning relationships with family, and clear cut findings concerning academic experiences and activities.

Most of the findings come from a follow-up survey carried out by the American Council on Higher Education. The survey was mailed in 1969 to 200,000 students who had earlier completed the ACE Student Information Form as entering freshmen in 1966, 1967, 1968, or 1969. The sample was drawn from 180 four-year colleges and universities and 65 two-year colleges which had turned in significant data for the freshman surveys. The size of the subsamples depended upon the size of the institution: at smaller institutions all previously surveyed students were sent the follow-up questionnaires;

at larger institutions random subsamples were drawn. Because it seemed likely that response rates would be higher for students with up-to-date addresses, maximum sample sizes also varied according to year of entrance: 300 students per institution for 1966, 275 for 1967, 250 for 1968, and 200 for 1969. The response rates were 38 percent for the 1966 and 1967 entrants, 41 percent for 1968 entrants, and 44 percent for 1969 entrants.

Analyses were restricted to the follow-up data for the 1966 freshmen. Three years later many of these students were in their junior or senior years. Others had completed a two-year college experience and transferred elsewhere. Still others had discontinued their education and were no longer in college. The item used to identify differences in residential status was this: "Where did you live most of the time during your most recent college term: college dormitory or other college-run housing, fraternity or sorority house, rooming house or rented room, apartment (not with parents or relatives), with parents or relatives, other?"

Findings are reported for respondents checking these alternatives: (a) "college dormitory or other college-run housing," (b) "rooming house or rented room," combined with "apartment (not with parents or relatives)," and (c) "with parents or relatives."

There is no guarantee, of course, that a student who lived with his parents or in a college dormitory during his most recent college term, had lived in that location during his full college experience. Therefore, these certainly are not pure subgroups. Surely, among the students in each group there are some who have moved from one residential setting to another, and perhaps a few who have lived under all three conditions. Despite all these uncontrolled factors, which must create a certain amount of "noise" in the underlying data, the results are sufficiently clear and sufficiently consistent with findings from other sources, that they provide convincing documentation for substantial differences in the college experiences of students who live at home with their parents, in private housing off campus, or in college dormitories.

The results from these analyses of the ACE survey are supplemented by findings from the Experience of College Questionnaire used in the context of the Project on Student Development in Small Colleges, a longitudinal study of institutional characteristics, student characteristics, attrition, and student development undertaken with the cooperation of thirteen liberal arts colleges, all with enrollments of 1500 or less. (For more detailed information see Chickering, 1969.) During the spring semester of 1967 the Experience of College Questionnaire was administered to stratified random samples of 150-200 students selected from all four grade levels to represent class size and the ratios of men and women within each class. Respondents were asked to indicate whether they were a "day student, living at home," or a "resident student, away from home." Analyses of the differences among these two groups were undertaken for five of the Project colleges. The results here are for commuters and residents aggregated from all five institutions.

Commuters who live with their parents more frequently flunk a course and are on academic probation; they less frequently take pass-fail courses or participate in an honors program or ROTC. They less frequently study less than five hours. Compared to dormitory residents, they less frequently do extra reading, check out a book or journal from the college library, study in the library, type a homework assignment, or argue with an instructor in class; they more frequently fail to complete an assignment on time and come late to class. They much less frequently discuss schoolwork with their friends or read books not required for courses. In general, therefore, the students who live at home with their parents appear to be less fully engaged in academic activities than their dormitory peers.

The students who live in private off-campus housing fall between the other two groups. There are significant exceptions, however, which are consistent with the special personal characteristics of many of these students. For example, these students more frequently argue with instructors in class and read books not required for courses. Although they flunk a course in about the same proportion as students who live at home, they take pass-fail courses at about the same rate as dormitory residents.

The findings from the Project on Student Development are consistent with the ACE survey results. Commuters do the assigned reading and take notes more consistently. They less frequently oversleep and miss a class. But, compared with residents, they coast more and are more often behind on their assignments.

Students who live at home have less contact with faculty

members than dormitory residents. They least frequently discuss topics in the professional field of their major professor or of other professors, and least frequently discuss other topics of intellectual interest or engage in social conversations. The differences between the commuters who live at home and those who live in private housing are again apparent in these data, where the latter group most frequently talked with their major professor about his field and had social conversations with him. The data from the small Project colleges suggest a more businesslike relationship between commuters and faculty, where commuters more frequently see the instructor in his office but are less frequently in his home and on a first name basis.

Students who live with their parents differ substantially from dormitory residents in their relationships with other students. Although all three groups reported similar numbers of close friends, commuters reported fewer close friends at their college and more close friends either at another college or not in college at all. Students who live with their parents least frequently join a fraternity or sorority and least frequently report having fallen in love—in contrast to commuters who live in private housing who are higher on both responses. On every item concerning social relationships with other students—dates, drinking beer, staying up all night, parties, hanging around a cafeteria, visiting a friend's apartment or room—commuters scored lower than dormitory residents. Students who live in private off-campus housing deviate in expected ways; they least frequently arrange dates for others, and most frequently drink beer, stay up all night, go out on dates, and attend parties.

The results from the Project colleges are again consistent with these ACE findings. Commuters were not as widely acquainted with other students and had fewer close friends at the college. They more frequently spend two hours or less in bull sessions, and less frequently spend five hours or more.

There are substantial differences between commuters and residents in extracurricular activities and experiences. On 24 of 27 items, commuters living at home scored lower than dormitory residents. The two major exceptions were playing chess and watching television. Significant differences occur for voting in student elections, working in political campaigns, and writing articles for school papers or magazines. Commuters living at home less frequently tutor minority group children, or participate in community organizations for social action. They least frequently read unassigned poetry, discuss religion, politics, or sports. Compared with dormitory residents, substantial proportions never in the course of their college career attend a meeting of some college organization, participate in student government, attend political meetings or lectures, or attend a concert, play, or art film.

What are commuters living at home doing instead of investing time in these varied extracurricular activities? Of course, many are spending time traveling back and forth to the college, and many are working. They also are watching television; 38.5 percent reported watching television once or twice a week, or nearly every day, compared with 23.6 percent of the dormitory residents.

These varied results unequivocally document widespread and substantial differences in the college experiences and activities of commuters and residents. In every area commuters are less involved than their resident peers. These differences begin in the freshman year and pervade the general college experience during the entire college period. The residents, who as entering freshmen bring wider ranging experiences and achievements and records of more effective academic performance, continue to exceed commuters in their level of participation. The freshmen who commute bring less competence, less experience, and a narrower range of achievements, and continue to operate in a more limited framework than the residents, missing the diverse possibilities that fuller and wider ranging participation offers.

# 7

# *Educational Consequences*

*W*hat happens to learning and personal development in residents and commuters when these different groups of students encounter the varied experiences and pursue the diverse activities of college?

In 1965 the American Council on Education began a research program which, as one of its major objectives, aimed to study how different college environments influence student development. Data were collected from freshmen when they first entered college and collected again from these same students at periodic intervals thereafter.

### Change During Freshman Year

The most comprehensive analyses of freshman year change were carried out with data from the follow-up survey of freshmen conducted in the fall of the following year. At the time of entrance these students completed a questionnaire of about 150 items and their colleges provided information about high school aptitude test scores. One year later those who had returned to school completed a mailed questionnaire, and their institutions supplied freshman grade point averages. The data for these longitudinal analyses came from the following institutions and students: 503 students from four public two-year colleges; 912 students from eight private two-year colleges; 1494 students from thirteen technological institutions; 2321 students from fifteen public four-year colleges; 3438 students from twenty-seven Roman Catholic four-year colleges; 4203 students from thirty Protestant four-year colleges; 6875 students from forty-three private nonsectarian four-year colleges; 3374 students from eighteen public universities; 3686 students from twenty-one private universities.

The first studies employed stepwise multiple regression analyses which revealed the directions of change for students living at home with their parents, in private off-campus housing, and in college dormitories. This approach uses responses to the initial questionnaire, which provided information about the student's high school, his family background, and his attitudes and activities, to predict his responses to the follow-up questionnaire. When the effects of the relationships between these background variables and follow-up items have been taken into account statistically, relationships between student changes and other variables concerning institutional characteristics or students' experiences can be studied. Three such variables describing living arrangements during the freshman year—"lived at home with parents," "lived in private home or apartment off campus," "lived in a college dormitory"—were examined in two different multiple regression analyses. One analysis studied changes in behaviors, the other studied changes in attitudes.

Each of these analyses also included items concerning future plans. Compared to residents, commuters—both those living at home and in private off-campus housing—less frequently plan to return to college and less frequently plan to study full time in their second year. Freshmen who had lived at home with their parents were less satisfied with college than either of the other two groups. These results, though simple, are of fundamental significance. If a freshman is so dissatisfied with his college experience that he does not return, then the college loses all opportunity for education and creates a negative background against which further educational efforts must work, should the student decide to try again elsewhere. Thus the commuter who drops out may not make even those gains achieved by his fellow commuters who persist, to say nothing of the gains made by his more fortunate residential counterparts.

There are consistent relationships between attitudes after the freshman year and living arrangements during that year. On every one of twelve different attitudes concerning social problems and college practices, students who live at home are more frequently conservative and those who live in college dormitories are more liberal. The differences between the two groups are especially large concerning freedom of speech, where commuters more frequently agree with policies restricting expression in the press and on the podium. Students living in private accommodations present a mixed picture, on some items responding more like dormitory students. Both commuter groups more frequently thought organized sports should be deemphasized, and students living in off-campus private housing much more frequently denied that their beliefs were similar to others.

There are consistently contrasting results in academic behaviors of students who lived at home and those who lived in college dormitories. Commuters, compared with residents, less frequently type homework, oversleep, ask teachers for advice, are guests in teachers' homes; they more frequently fail to complete homework assignments. On four of five items concerning activities with other students, commuters living at home scored lower than residents.

Students who live at home also consistently participate less frequently in varied kinds of organized demonstrations, and less frequently discuss religion and politics. Commuters see foreign movies less frequently but visit art galleries more frequently than residents; they also ride motorcycles and get traffic tickets much more frequently than residents.

Most of these differences occurred at high levels of statistical significance and indicate how substantially changes in behaviors during the freshman year differ when students who lived at home are compared with their peers who had lived in college dormitories.

The changes in these behaviors are consistent with the changes in attitudes that characterize the two groups. Commuters have less contact with faculty members and are less involved in varied activities with fellow students. They discuss politics and religion less frequently and participate in demonstrations less often.

At the same time, after a year in college their attitudes toward sociopolitical issues are more frequently conservative than the attitudes of fellow freshmen who had lived in dormitories.

Data concerning self-perceptions and long range goals were also assembled. Stepwise multiple regression analyses were employed for these data, but in this case students who lived at home with their parents were the only subgroup examined. Responses to nineteen items report the relationship between living at home and changes in self-perceptions and in long range goals. On fourteen of the items the the relationships between living at home during the freshman year and self-perceptions at the end of that year are negative. All four of the statistically significant items are negative: public speaking ability, leadership ability, social self-confidence, and popularity. Artistic ability, intellectual self-confidence, and popularity with the opposite sex, show substantial, but nonsignificant negative relationships. All five of the positive items, while they are in the plus direction, are very close to zero.

In general, therefore, after differences in background characteristics and differences in self-perceptions at entrance are taken into account, students who live at home during the freshman year rate themselves lower on many important characteristics and abilities, than students who live under other conditions. Thus, during the freshman year, the self-esteem of these commuting students suffers in comparison with their residential peers.

These shifts in self-esteem are accompanied by similar shifts in long range goals. Students who live at home rate eleven of sixteen long range goals less important at the end of their freshman year, than do their other freshman peers; all three of the statistically significant relationships—"becoming accomplished in the performing arts," "doing a great artistic work," and "becoming a community leader"—are negative. In general therefore, at the same time that the self-esteem for students who had lived at home suffered in comparison with their fellow students in other living arrangements, their commitments to a wide range of long range goals diminished.

Because they are so consistent, the results from the varied multiple regression analyses of change during the freshman year are easily summarized. It is important to remember that statistical controls were exercised, which take into account numerous differences between the groups—differences in high school and family backgrounds as well as differences in the items themselves which were readministered to assess change. After one year in college, when compared with students who live in college dormitories, students who live at home with their parents are less fully involved in academic activities and in extra-curricular activities with other students, rate themselves lower on a variety of abilities and desirable personal characteristics, are less committed to a diverse array of long range goals, and are more conservative in their sociopolitical attitudes.

These results suggested that more detailed studies comparing actual scores with predicted scores would be useful. These analyses were carried out for 26,806 students and 179 institutions. Regression analyses predicted a score for each student on eighty-five different variables from the questionnaire completed at entrance and from information provided by the institutions. A student's actual score when he completed the second questionnaire in the fall of the following year was then compared with his predicted score and a difference score was generated. Then correlational analyses, carried out with a randomly selected subsample of 6701 respondents, examined the differences between predicted and actual scores for students who live at home with their parents, those who live in private off-campus housing, and those who live in college dormitories.

One analysis examined a variety of competence items and found a striking internal consistency among them within each living group. In all but two cases actual scores were *lower* than predicted scores for students who live with their parents, and actual scores were *higher* than predicted scores for students who live in college dormitories. These changes occurred even though the *predicted scores* in every case were *lower for students living at home* and *higher for dormitory students*. The differences in predicted scores arose primarily from the fact that at entrance the dormitory students more frequently demonstrated these competencies than students living at home.

To put it briefly then, at entrance, dormitory students report a wider range of competence than students living with parents; during the freshman year the range for dormitory students expanded and the range for commuters living at home shrank. Thus these two groups of students, coming from different educational and family backgrounds, move farther apart rather than closer together.

Two exceptions are worth noting for the ring of truth they add. Students who live at home report competence in sewing and baking more often than students who spend the year in a dormitory. As in most of the previous analyses, students who live in private accommodations off campus fall between the other two groups. Their scores drop consistently for the five sport items; they rise for activities they are best positioned to pursue—"partying," "sewing," and "baking."

The findings for various behavior items are consistent with those for competence. For all but three items—"visited an art gallery or museum," "rode on a motorcycle," "got a traffic ticket"—predicted scores for dormitory students are higher than for students living with parents. And on fourteen of the nineteen behaviors, actual scores for home-dwellers fell short of predicted scores, while actual scores for residents were higher. The home-dwellers tutored and studied with other students less frequently than predicted, in contrast to residents. Similar results occurred for discussing religion, seeing foreign movies, taking a trip, and participating in demonstrations. Commuters were less frequently a guest in a teacher's home.

Generally then, at entrance commuters are less disposed than residents to enter various educationally and developmentally useful activities and experiences. During the freshman year the differences between these groups grows, as participation by resident students exceeds predictions and as students living at home participate less than predicted.

Once again, students living in private off-campus housing presented a mixed picture in attitudes, falling usually between dormitory students and students living at home. Table 5 gives the attitude items which yielded statistically significant correlation coefficients for one or more of the groups.

Table 6 gives the findings for some additional variables of interest. Students in private off-campus housing differed from the other two groups on college grade point average (GPA), their scores increasing beyond predictions, while the others, especially the dormitory residents, dropped. But both kinds of commuters differed significantly from the residents in satisfaction with their colleges and in their plans to return and to study full time, reporting decreased satisfaction and less likelihood of returning for full-time study than predicted on the basis of their entering characteristics.

These various studies of change among commuters and residents during the freshman year produced remarkably consistent results. Students who lived at home with their parents, in comparison with those who lived in college dormitories, had been less fully involved in academic activities, had participated less frequently in extra-curricular activities with other students, had entered educationally and developmentally useful experiences and activities less frequently, reported fewer areas of competence, rated themselves lower on a variety of abilities and desirable personal characteristics, were less committed to a diverse array of long range goals, were less satisfied with college and less likely to return.

## Change After Four Years

Data concerning change after four years are from the 1969 ACE survey sent to students who completed the ACE freshman survey in 1966, 1967, and 1968, and from the 1970 ACE follow-up survey sent to 1966 freshmen. For purposes of this study, data from the survey were analyzed for the 1966 entrants only. Most of these students completed the survey in December or January of 1969. Therefore those who were still in four-year institutions and had followed the usual timetable were in the first half of their senior year. Those who had entered two-year colleges and graduated on schedule were either at work or in a similar stage in the four-year institution to which they had transferred. Some of the respondents had dropped out of either the two-year or four-year institutions in which they had enrolled in the freshman survey and were no longer in college. Thus these Carnegie findings combine several different types of respondents—those near the end of a regular four-year program, those who had moved into a four-year program from a two-year college, those who had graduated from two-year colleges and had gone to work, and those who had dropped out and had not returned.

Each respondent was asked where he lived most of the time

## Table 5.

## EFFECTS OF RESIDENTIAL STATUS ON ATTITUDES
## AMONG FRESHMEN 1967–68

| | WITH PARENTS | | |
|---|---|---|---|
| Outcome Measure | $R^a$ | Actual | Predicted |
| Married women belong at home | —.005 | 2.389 | 2.356 |
| College has right to ban extremists | .040* | 2.079 | 1.997 |
| College faculty should specify curriculum | .026* | 2.930 | 2.890 |
| Organized sports should be de-emphasized | .032* | 1.901 | 1.867 |
| My beliefs are similar to other students | —.020 | 2.642 | 2.640 |

| | PRIVATE OFF-CAMPUS | | |
|---|---|---|---|
| Outcome Measure | $R$ | Actual | Predicted |
| Married women belong at home | —.029* | 2.322 | 2.354 |
| College has right to ban extremists | —.011 | 1.990 | 1.996 |
| College faculty should specify curriculum | .007 | 2.903 | 2.879 |
| Organized sports should be de-emphasized | .013 | 2.081 | 1.978 |
| My beliefs are similar to other students | —.026* | 2.497 | 2.592 |

| | COLLEGE DORMITORY | | |
|---|---|---|---|
| Outcome Measure | $R$ | Actual | Predicted |
| Married women belong at home | .019 | 2.126 | 2.125 |
| College has right to ban extremists | —.030* | 1.781 | 1.788 |
| College faculty should specify curriculum | —.016 | 2.825 | 2.824 |
| Organized sports should be de-emphasized | —.022 | 1.980 | 1.986 |
| My beliefs are similar to other students | .033* | 2.598 | 2.574 |

[a] After control of student input variables including Outcome Measures.

* — $p < .05$

Note: Effects of residential status on each outcome are determined by first partialing out the effects of student input variables. Responses scored 1—Disagree Strongly, 2—Disagree Somewhat, 3—Agree Somewhat, 4—Agree Strongly.

## Table 6.

### EFFECTS OF RESIDENTIAL STATUS ON GRADE POINT AVERAGE, SATISFACTION, AND PERSISTENCE AMONG FRESHMEN 1967–68

| Outcome Measure | WITH PARENTS | | |
| --- | --- | --- | --- |
| | $R^a$ | Actual | Predicted |
| College GPA | .022 | 3.574 | 3.582 |
| Overall satisfaction with the college | −.031* | 3.801 | 3.852 |
| Will be full-time student in 1968 | −.046* | 1.906 | 1.922 |
| Plan to return to same college in 1968 | −.074* | 1.800 | 1.824 |
| Participation in demonstration against administrative policy | −.036* | 1.112 | 1.132 |
| Participation in demonstrations against Vietnam war | −.002 | 1.052 | 1.065 |

| Outcome Measure | PRIVATE OFF-CAMPUS | | |
| --- | --- | --- | --- |
| | $R$ | Actual | Predicted |
| College GPA | .019 | 3.561 | 3.412 |
| Overall satisfaction with the college | −.034* | 3.796 | 3.808 |
| Will be full-time student in 1968 | −.081* | 1.827 | 1.887 |
| Plan to return to same college in 1968 | −.077* | 1.678 | 1.798 |
| Participation in demonstration against administrative policy | −.000 | 1.117 | 1.146 |
| Participation in demonstrations against Vietnam war | .025* | 1.113 | 1.081 |

| Outcome Measure | COLLEGE DORMITORY | | |
| --- | --- | --- | --- |
| | $R$ | Actual | Predicted |
| College GPA | −.039 | 3.810 | 3.849 |
| Overall satisfaction with the college | .015 | 3.989 | 3.954 |
| Will be full-time student in 1968 | .056* | 1.966 | 1.954 |
| Plan to return to same college in 1968 | .007 | 1.877 | 1.851 |
| Participation in demonstration against administrative policy | .044* | 1.185 | 1.175 |
| Participation in demonstrations against Vietnam war | −.004 | 1.109 | 1.116 |

[a] After control of student input variables including Outcome Measures.
\* = $p < .05$
Note: Effects of residential status on each outcome are determined by first partialling out the effects of student input variables. GPA responses coded as 8 ("A or A+"), 7 ("A—"), 6 ("B+"), 5 ("B"), 4 ("B—"), 3 ("C+"), 2 ("C"), 1 ("D"). College Evaluation responses coded 5 (Very satisfied with my college), 4 (Satisfied with my college), 3 (On the fence), 2 (Dissatisfied with my college), 1 (Very dissatisfied with my college).

during his most recent college term. The data were analyzed separately for students who checked one of three residences: "college dormitory or other college run housing," "with parents or relatives," and "rooming house or rented room, apartment (not with parents or relatives)." The differences among these three groups are consistent with the differences to be expected given their entering characteristics and the changes evidenced during their first year in college.

The respondents were asked their goals in regard to the academic degree they wished to achieve. About 14 percent of the students who live at home intend to obtain an associate degree or no degree at all, compared with 3 percent of those living in other private housing, and 9 percent of the resident students. Thirty-nine percent of the resident students intend to obtain master's degrees compared with 30 percent of those who live with parents. About 16 percent of the students living in other private housing aim for "other professional" degrees, in contrast to only 10 percent of the other two groups. Interestingly, the proportions who aim for a Ph.D. or Ed.D. Degree are roughly equal.

The career expectations and preferences differ for the three groups. Students who live with their parents more frequently expect careers in engineering and the sciences and less frequently expect careers in teaching, psychology, or social welfare. Students who live in other private housing more frequently expect careers in law, college teaching, and as a business executive, official, or owner. Dormitory students show the highest proportion for secondary and elementary teaching, and for housewifery.

The housewife responses are worth noting. In all three groups about half as many persons prefer that career as expect to pursue it. Because the total number of respondents were about evenly divided between men and women, the percentage figures should be doubled to indicate the proportions of women who checked that item. Therefore, for example, about 20 percent of the women who live at home with their parents expect the career of housewife, even though only 10 percent prefer that career; about 10 percent of the women who live in other private housing expect that career while only about 5 percent prefer it.

Although there were not dramatic differences among the

groups, the data concerning long range goals are consistent with the differences in degree and career plans. Students who live with their parents more frequently rate being successful in a business of their own and being very well off financially as important or somewhat important; students living in other off-campus housing more frequently want to influence the political structure and social values and least frequently give priority to having an active social life; dormitory residents frequently rate "becoming a community leader" or "accomplished in the performing arts" as important long range goals.

These varied findings concerning plans and aspirations are consistent with their degree plans. Commuters who live at home with their parents more frequently intend to obtain an associate degree, a bachelor's degree, or no degree at all and less frequently aimed for master's degrees. Students who lived in other off-campus housing, and dormitory residents, much less frequently intend to obtain associate degrees and, more frequently than students who live at home, aim for master's degrees. Students who live at home expect careers in engineering and the sciences, which do not necessarily require master's degrees and which lead to higher incomes than their dormitory peers who more frequently expect to teach and recognize the value of a master's degree for that profession. Students in private off-campus housing also recognize the need for master's degrees to pursue their expected careers as lawyers, college teachers, or business executives, and to implement their long range concerns to influence political and social structures.

It is not surprising that differences in self-concept accompany these differences in career plans and aspirations. On six of eight skills—academic, writing, artistic, public speaking, leadership, athletic—dormitory students rate themselves higher than either group of commuters. On five of the skills—academic, writing, public speaking, leadership, athletic—students who live at home rank themselves lowest. On each of the additional personal characteristics —intellectual and social self confidence, popularity, understanding others, sensitivity to criticism, defensiveness, stubbornness, cheerfulness—residents ranked themselves highest. The consistency among these diverse items, evidenced in past patterns as well, is striking. Furthermore, it is important to recognize that the cumulative conse-

## Table 7.

ATTITUDES TOWARD HIGHER EDUCATION
1966 FRESHMEN RE-SURVEYED IN DECEMBER, 1969

| | Residential Status | | |
|---|---|---|---|
| Outcome Measure | With Parents | Other Private | College Dormitory |
| I Agree That: | | | |
| Student demonstrations have no place on a college campus. | 37.1 | 21.2 | 24.4 |
| Students who disrupt the functioning of a college should be expelled or suspended. | 69.5 | 55.7 | 58.7 |
| Political activities by students have no place on a college campus. | 21.8 | 9.5 | 11.4 |
| Most college officials have been too lax in dealing with student protesters on campus. | 54.1 | 42.1 | 47.3 |
| Student publications should be cleared by college officials. | 44.3 | 25.0 | 32.7 |
| Undergraduates known to use marijuana regularly should be suspended or dismissed. | 33.6 | 23.4 | 32.8 |
| The chief benefit of a college education is that it increases one's earning power. | 52.1 | 41.7 | 41.7 |
| Faculty members should be free on campus to advocate violent resistance to public authority. | 24.1 | 41.1 | 31.0 |
| Most American colleges and universities are racist whether they mean to be or not. | 33.3 | 47.1 | 45.1 |
| Any special academic program for black students should be administered and controlled by black people. | 40.4 | 49.3 | 43.3 |

*Table 7. (cont.)*

ATTITUDES TOWARD HIGHER EDUCATION
1966 FRESHMEN RE-SURVEYED IN DECEMBER, 1969

| | Residential Status | | |
| Outcome Measure | With Parents | Other Private | College Dormitory |
| --- | --- | --- | --- |
| Faculty promotions should be based on student evaluations. | 38.7 | 48.2 | 47.8 |
| A strike would be a legitimate means of collective action for faculty members under some circumstances. | 63.7 | 68.8 | 62.3 |
| Most American colleges reward conformity and crush student creativity. | 48.9 | 61.1 | 56.2 |
| Students should have a role in specifying the college curriculum. | 69.1 | 72.8 | 73.7 |

*Note:* Figures are percentages responding to indicated option.

quences across diverse areas may have substantially greater implications for sense of competence and self-esteem than the small differences within each item might suggest.

Attitudes toward higher education, Table 7, reflect consistent and substantial differences between students who live at home and those who live in private off-campus housing. Commuters from home are consistently more conservative and oriented toward law, order, censorship, clear control by authority, and punitive measures. Students who live in off-campus housing are much more frequently civil-libertarian and activist in orientation. The attitudes of dormitory students are more frequently similar to those of private housing students, although their responses are less internally consistent than the other two groups.

Similar differences among the groups occur for a wide range of other attitudes and beliefs concerning political processes, domestic priorities, legal issues, and international relations as well as civil liberties and racial integration. Home-dwellers consistently agree with conservative positions more frequently than either of the other two groups, and students who live in private housing consistently agree more frequently with liberal orientations. Again the figures for dormitory students tend to fall between the other two groups. These data reporting various attitudes and beliefs concerning higher education and sociopolitical issues clearly document substantial differences among the commuters who live at home, those who live in private off-campus housing, and dormitory residents. These differences after four years—in degree and career plans, in long range goals, in self-perceptions, in attitudes and beliefs—are consistent with the characteristics of these different groups at entrance and consistent with the directions of change observed after the first year (Table 8).

*Table 8.*

GENERAL ATTITUDES AND BELIEFS
1966 FRESHMEN RE-SURVEYED IN DECEMBER, 1969

| | Residential Status | | |
|---|---|---|---|
| Outcome Measure | With Parents | Other Private | College Dormitory |
| I Agree That: | | | |
| *Political Processes* | | | |
| In the USA today there can be no justification for using violence to achieve political goals. | 79.2 | 68.3 | 73.6 |
| Meaningful social change cannot be achieved through traditional American politics. | 46.6 | 54.2 | 50.9 |
| *Civil Liberties* | | | |
| There is too much concern in the courts for the rights of criminals. | 42.6 | 34.5 | 36.6 |
| Man will never realize his potential until he is freed from the laws and conventions of society. | 25.9 | 34.4 | 27.3 |

*Table 8 (cont.)*

GENERAL ATTITUDES AND BELIEFS
1966 FRESHMEN RE-SURVEYED IN DECEMBER, 1969

| | Residential Status | | |
|---|---|---|---|
| Outcome Measure | With Parents | Other Private | College Dormitory |
| Only volunteers should serve in the armed forces. | 66.4 | 76.0 | 65.1 |
| Scientists should publish their findings regardless of the possible consequences. | 66.0 | 69.5 | 64.2 |
| *Racial Integration* | | | |
| These days you hear too much about the rights of minorities and not enough about the rights of the majority. | 59.4 | 44.8 | 52.3 |
| The main cause of Negro riots in the cities in white racism. | 40.7 | 52.0 | 46.5 |
| Where *de facto* segregation exists, black people should be assured control over their own schools. | 63.5 | 74.4 | 71.7 |
| Racial integration of the public elementary schools should be achieved even if it requires busing. | 45.4 | 51.1 | 46.0 |
| *Domestic Priorities* | | | |
| However acute our domestic problems, we cannot afford to suspend our space effort. | 54.5 | 42.4 | 46.2 |
| Most people who live in poverty could do something about their situation if they really wanted to. | 61.4 | 43.0 | 51.9 |

*Table 8 (cont.)*

GENERAL ATTITUDES AND BELIEFS
1966 FRESHMEN RE-SURVEYED IN DECEMBER, 1969

| Outcome Measure | Residential Status | | |
| --- | --- | --- | --- |
| | With Parents | Other Private | College Dormitory |
| Urban problems cannot be solved without huge investments of Federal money. | 64.0 | 69.4 | 67.9 |
| Current levels of air pollution in large cities justify the use of drastic measures to limit the use of motor vehicles. | 63.9 | 70.5 | 63.7 |
| *Legal Issues* | | | |
| Cigarette advertising should be outlawed. | 60.3 | 55.4 | 53.6 |
| Capital punishment (the death penalty) should be abolished. | 53.4 | 66.0 | 62.7 |
| Marijuana should be legalized. | 46.5 | 62.7 | 48.3 |
| Divorce laws should be liberalized. | 52.2 | 65.3 | 53.3 |
| Under some conditions, abortions should be legalized. | 88.1 | 92.8 | 86.9 |
| *International Affairs* | | | |
| Some form of Communist regime is probably necessary for progress in underdeveloped countries. | 30.1 | 41.3 | 34.0 |
| Communist China should be recognized immediately by the U. S. | 55.9 | 63.5 | 56.7 |
| The U. S. should withdraw from Vietnam immediately. | 59.3 | 67.5 | 61.0 |

*Note:* Figures are percentages responding to indicated option.

Although this combination of findings is persuasive, we cannot yet conclude that these differences after four years are a consequence of the differences in college experiences and activities that characterize these three types of residential arrangements. Those conclusions must rest on evidence that clearly takes account of the differences among the groups as entering freshmen, because differences in change may be much more a function of those initial characteristics than of the college experiences themselves.

The multiple regression analyses undertaken with the ACE follow-up data of the freshman respondents four years later takes account of those background differences and reveals the extent to which changes may be attributed to the college experiences themselves, above and beyond the changes that would be predicted simply on the basis of the differences in backgrounds, abilities, values, and interests that were evident as entering freshmen.

Resident students surveyed four years after the initial questioning consistently exceed predictions in planning for an associate in arts or bachelor of arts degrees, and in planning for degrees higher than the associate in arts. Commuters who live with their parents with equal consistency fall short of predictions concerning their degree plans. Commuters living in private off-campus housing also fall short of predictions based on their background characteristics, especially with reference to aspirations beyond the associate in arts degree. Thus, even when the differences in academic preparation and background in abilities, values, and interests of commuters and residents are taken into account in predicting degree plans, commuters fall short of those predictions and residents exceed them.

When long range plans are considered in more detail, interesting differences between commuters who live at home and those who live in private off-campus housing emerge. Commuters who live at home shift to greater emphasis on financial well being. Being well off financially seems to be the dominant aspect of their shifting orientation, which is accompanied by "becoming an expert in finance and commerce" and "never being obligated to people." These students shift away from concern about keeping up to date with political affairs and with concern for creating artistic works. For commuters living in private off-campus housing the dominant shifts reflect primarily a concern for independence, where not being obligated is combined with much stronger emphasis either on being successful in a business of their own, or in creating artistic works, both of which accompany a shift away from simple concern about being well off financially. The pattern for resident students is still different, reflecting diminished concern for financial well being, business success, and obligations to others, and increased orientation to artistic creativity, social contributions through the Peace Corps, and keeping up to date with political affairs.

Students were surveyed on changes in self-perceptions which accompanied these changing degree plans and long range goals. Commuters who live with their parents rank themselves lower than predicted on academic ability and leadership ability. They also rank themselves lower on self-confidence, social self-confidence, popularity in general, and popularity with the opposite sex. Given these shifting self-perceptions it is not surprising that they also are the only group that rank themselves lower on "cheerfulness," and significantly so. Nor is it surprising that given these shifts in self-perception their degree aspirations drop and their long range goals narrow to simple financial security, goals that can be met by relying on their more positive self-ratings on mathematical ability and mechanical ability.

The commuters who lived in private off-campus housing contrast sharply with those who lived at home. They rank themselves significantly higher than predicted on academic ability, artistic ability, mathematical ability, and mechanical ability. They also rank themselves higher on intellectual and social self-confidence and on popularity with the opposite sex, and lower on "drive to achieve." With increased sense of competence and self-confidence across a wide range of areas, it is not surprising that they also rank themselves higher than predictions on "cheerfulness." Such changes in self-esteem support their long range plans, which combine more frequent orientation toward independence and self-sufficiency with more frequent interest in artistic creativity.

The dormitory residents' self-ratings shift in a pattern that tends to be a counterpoint to the commuters who live at home. They rank themselves significantly lower than predicted on mathematical and mechanical ability, and on leadership ability, and higher on sensitivity to criticism. They rank themselves significantly higher on popularity and on social self-confidence. Rankings on academic ability and intellectual self-confidence show little change, however.

Commuters who live at home, who tend to be conservative as entering freshmen, rank themselves as conservative even more frequently and liberal even less frequently, four years later. Students who live in private off-campus housing, and dormitory residents, more frequently call themselves liberals and not conservatives.

These changes in degree plans, in long range plans, and in self-perceptions are consistent with the shifts in behaviors reflected by reports from the students as freshmen and four years later (see Table 9). There are dramatic and highly consistent contrasts between students who live at home and those who live in college

*Table 9.*

EFFECTS OF RESIDENTIAL STATUS ON BEHAVIOR
1966 FRESHMEN RE-SURVEYED IN 1970

| | Residential Status | | |
| --- | --- | --- | --- |
| Outcome Measure | Lived With Parents | Other Private Home or Apartment | College Dormitory |
| *Activities with Peers* | | | |
| Argued with friends | Negative† | Negative* | Positive† |
| Participated in organized demonstration | Negative† | Positive$^{n.s.}$ | Positive† |
| Discussed how to make money with friends | Positive* | Positive$^{n.s.}$ | Negative$^{n.s.}$ |
| Arranged a date for a friend | Negative** | Negative† | Positive† |
| Had a blind date | Negative† | Negative† | Positive† |
| Went to movies | Negative$^{n.s.}$ | Negative$^{n.s.}$ | Positive** |
| Went to overnight or weekend party | Negative† | Negative† | Positive† |
| Drank beer | Negative† | Negative† | Positive† |
| Stayed up all night | Negative† | Negative$^{n.s.}$ | Positive* |
| Drank wine | Negative† | Positive$^{n.s.}$ | Positive† |
| Participated in informal group activity | Negative† | Negative† | Positive† |

*Table 9. (cont.)*

### Effects of Residential Status on Behavior
### 1966 Freshmen Re-Surveyed in 1970

| Outcome Measure | Residential Status | | |
| --- | --- | --- | --- |
| | Lived With Parents | Other Private Home or Apartment | College Dormitory |
| *Cultural Activities* | | | |
| Listened to folk music | Negative$^\dagger$ | Positive$^{n.s.}$ | Positive$^*$ |
| Listened to social music | Negative$^{**}$ | Negative$^{n.s.}$ | Positive$^\dagger$ |
| Listened to rock music | Negative$^*$ | Negative$^{**}$ | Positive$^{**}$ |
| Played a musical instrument | Negative$^*$ | Negative$^{n.s.}$ | Negative$^{n.s.}$ |
| Attended a ballet performance | Negative$^\dagger$ | Negative$^{n.s.}$ | Positive$^\dagger$ |
| Attended a public recital or concert | Negative$^\dagger$ | Negative$^*$ | Positive$^\dagger$ |
| *Religious Activities* | | | |
| Attended Church | Positive$^\dagger$ | Negative$^\dagger$ | Negative$^{n.s.}$ |
| Attended Sunday School | Positive$^\dagger$ | Positive$^{n.s.}$ | Negative$^\dagger$ |
| Said grace before meals | Positive$^\dagger$ | Negative$^{**}$ | Negative$^\dagger$ |
| Prayed | Positive$^\dagger$ | Negative$^\dagger$ | Negative$^\dagger$ |
| *Miscellaneous Activities* | | | |
| Overslept and missed a class or appointment | Negative$^\dagger$ | Negative$^{n.s.}$ | Positive$^\dagger$ |
| Took a nap or rest during the day | Negative$^\dagger$ | Negative$^\dagger$ | Positive$^\dagger$ |
| Drove a car | Positive$^\dagger$ | Positive$^{n.s.}$ | Negative$^\dagger$ |
| Smoked cigarettes | Negative$^\dagger$ | Positive$^{n.s.}$ | Positive$^\dagger$ |

*Note:* Effects of residential status on each outcome are determined
by first partialling out the effects of student input variables.

n.s. = non-significant

$^*$ = $p < .05$

$^{**}$ = $p < .01$

$^\dagger$ = $p < .001$

dormitories. The students who live in other private housing, as has usually been the case, show behaviors much more like the students living at home than like the resident students.

In a series of eleven activities, which typically involve social relationships with other students or persons of similar age, students who live with their parents participated in ten less frequently than predicted on the basis of their background characteristics, and students who live in college dormitories participate more frequently than predicted. The one exception was "discussed how to make money with friends" where commuters exceed predictions. In a series of six cultural activities, commuters fall below and residents exceed predictions on five. The single exception is "played a musical instrument" where commuters exceed predictions. Commuters exceed predictions at high levels of statistical significance for four religious activities, while residents significantly fall below predictions. The contrasting patterns persist for a series of miscellaneous activities as well.

Perhaps the most striking thing about these diverse studies is the consistency of the results. Whatever the institution, whatever the group, whatever the data, whatever the methods of analyses, the findings are the same. Students who live at home with their parents fall short of the kinds of learning and personal development typically desired by the institutions they attend and which might reasonably be expected when their special backgrounds are taken into account. Students who live in college dormitories exceed the learning and personal development that are predicted when their advantages in ability, in prior educational and extracurricular activities, and in community and family backgrounds are taken into account. During the freshman year and during all four years for several different large samples, examined through simple retest comparisons and through complex multivariate analyses, the findings remain consistent.

Students who live at home, in comparison with those who live in college dormitories, are less fully involved in academic activities, in extracurricular activities, and in social activities with other students. Their degree aspirations diminish and they become less committed to a variety of long range goals. They enter educationally and developmentally useful experiences and activities less frequently.

They report a shrinking range of competence. Their self-ratings for a diverse array of abilities and desirable personal characteristics drop. Their satisfaction with college decreases, and they become less likely to return.

Commuters and residents begin their college careers with an unequal start which strongly favors the residents. The gap between them grows. Residents have access to, find, and are forced to encounter diverse experiences and persons who spur them on their way. Access, discovery, and encounter occur much less for commuters and they continue in circumstances that add weights to their preexisting handicaps. Thus the major consequence of American higher education as it currently functions for commuters and residents is to increase the distance between them.

Unto them that hath is given. From them that hath not, is taken away.

# 8

# *Matching College to Student*

$\mathcal{S}$everal sociopsychological concepts provide a rationale for action aimed at reducing the inequities in the college experience of commuters and resident students and for the recommendations offered in the next chapter.

## Identification with Individuals and with Reference Groups

Relationships with other persons exert the most powerful influences on individual development—relationships with parents during childhood and early adolescence, relationships with close friends, working colleagues, and various adult groups after that. These relationships filter and modify the messages from the larger culture, they amplify or dampen the pressures of various social forces and expectations. The principal reason that different college environments, different living arrangements, different procedures for curriculum, teaching, and evaluation have varied impacts, is that they influence the individuals and groups with which students become associated.

Case studies and statistical analyses have documented the impact of close friendships during the college years. Davie (1958) wrote of the influence of close friends on overall development, particularly on autonomy and identity. Dressel and Lehmann (1965) analyzed the influence of roommates and residence hall associates on attitudes and values. Newcomb (1961, 1962) and Newcomb and Feldman (1968) studied the forces generated by shared interests and values. White (1958) wrote of the impact on vocational plans and aspirations, and on freeing interpersonal relationships in his book *Lives in Progress*.

Wallace (1966) found that close friendships principally exert influence on fundamental developmental issues not only in the transitional life of a student in college, but also in developing an orientation to life in general, to adulthood, life goals, parents, religion, sex, politics.

Thus, the inner circle of close friends exerts direct and forceful influence on the student. Daily behavior is influenced by their needs and interests. Unassigned books read are those close friends recommend and assigned readings thoughtfully examined and discussed are those that have proven thought provoking for friends whose reactions are respected. Television viewing, trips taken, topics for reflection, styles of dress, all similarly respond to these close friendships.

Often the influence of such friends is enlarged and enriched by the values, standards and interests of groups to which they belong. The conceptual framework developed by Sherif and Sherif (1964) in their research on reference groups clarifies the dynamics by which groups influence their members. It is directly pertinent to the differences in college experiences and educational outcomes for commuters and residents, and the comments which follow borrow freely from the Sherif and Sherif report.

Human beings establish strong social ties with others for two reasons. First, these social ties provide a dependable basis for a stable self-concept, a firm sense of identity. Although over a period of time major personality changes may occur, the day-to-day feedback from trusted friends gives a sense of personal constancy even while change is occurring. Second, these social ties provide both direct assistance in the business of living and in emotional support when problems arise or when new and different experiences must be met. The social ties that serve these functions are often linked with membership in groups—informal friendship groups or more formal structures in work, community activities, clubs.

Once a person identifies himself with a group that group becomes an anchor and a reference point. The values and behaviors approved by the group provide the background for developing individual attitudes and behaviors. When a person is strongly identified with a group the shared standards and rules for conduct are not felt to be arbitrary, capricious, or meaningless; they are not seen as coercive, restricting, or authoritarian. Because members of the group share and have an investment in the group's norms and expectations, sanctions and pressures in response to deviance are applied by everyone and not simply by a single leader or official. Indeed the formal or informal leaders of the group themselves are not immune to such reactions. Loyalty to the group and what it stands for supercedes loyalty to individuals within it.

Such reference groups develop when associations are frequent, long-lasting, or both; when members face common problems, share common tasks, or otherwise engage in meaningful activities together; when status and roles are varied enough so that longevity of association and being a good member is rewarded and recognized; and when the boundaries with respect to other groups or organizations are reasonably clear so that one knows who is in and who is out. As a group becomes important the individual tries to maintain and strengthen his position in it by behaving appropriately and by demonstrating the competencies relevant to the group's needs and to the members' values.

The extent to which a new group can assume force for an individual depends on two things. First, it depends upon how much the ties to other social structures have been disrupted, the ties to family, to friends, to associates at work or in the community, to other significant reference groups. And second, it depends upon how much the new group helps the individual fulfill his social, emotional, and material needs, upon how much it helps him realize his immediate purposes or helps him move toward more long range objectives.

The implications of reference group theory for the research results concerning commuters and residents are obvious, as they are for many of the findings concerning college impacts on student development. For resident students there is a clear and sharp break

with family, friends, social ties, and the reference groups with which
they were closely identified during the high school years. Furthermore, they move into a college they choose from a fairly wide range
of alternatives. They choose it because they have heard things about
it which they like from others, or because they have been there
themselves and are attracted by the persons they meet and what they
see or hear. So they are moving toward persons and subcultures
with which they are predisposed and often very eager to identify.
Many entering freshmen adopt the dress styles, language, eating
and sleeping habits, and other behavior patterns which characterize
the institution or subculture they select, with amazing speed, sensitivity, and flexibility. Often within two or three weeks the surface
behaviors of a first semester freshman are hard to distinguish from
the returning pace-setters. Often there is a susceptibility and
vulnerability to exploitation by upper classmen during these early
weeks that is greater than at any other period. This vulnerability
usually has become tempered by the end of the freshman year as the
significant individual and subcultural differences that lie beneath the
surface are more clearly perceived, and as the individual, after
gaining acceptance, is able to express more openly past attitudes,
interests, and actions that are still significant for him.

The commuting student who lives at home with his parents,
however, has not chosen his college from a wide range of alternatives
and experiences no clear break or disruption with his past friendships and reference groups. Often he applied only to the college he
is attending, and did so because it is the only one that is available
to him for reasons of finance, employment, or family responsibilities.
He has not, therefore, been attracted to it in the same way that the
resident student was, nor has he identified in it particular elements
to which he is strongly drawn. Many of his friends in high school or
on the job persist, as do his identifications with various groups that
are important to him. There are fewer openings through which new
friendships can be established and for investment in or identification
with new groups. And furthermore, there is not the opportunity for
the frequent and intensive interpersonal contact that can accelerate
that identification.

Therefore, his identification with the institution will occur
much more gradually, if it occurs at all. High school friends and

groups may gradually break up. If he has a job, the time and energy needed for study will cut into former friendships and activities. Former friends may gradually be replaced by persons he meets in various classes, in the library, or in other college activities. After a year or so his parents also may become more adjusted to his new routines, and his disengagement from them may have gained sufficient momentum to permit more open and flexible adoption of new friends, new activities, and new styles.

One way, therefore, to help commuting students get a faster start and to close somewhat the gap between commuters and residents in educational outcomes, is to accelerate the opportunities for discovering and identifying with new reference groups which are more pertinent to their future plans and aspirations and less related to the self-perceptions and expectations of the cultures from which these students come.

## Individual Differences

What determines whether or not a particular experience has an impact on interpersonal relationships, whether or not it provokes increased gaps between individuals or enables increased integration? An important part of the answer lies in the characteristics of the individuals concerned. When individuals differ, a single experience can have diverse outcomes. The impact on the student of a given curriculum, course, teacher, fellow student, or residence hall experience will vary depending upon the background of the student. Despite the fact that this principle smacks us in the eye daily, higher education has given little attention to it. Instead, students have been treated as though they were billiard balls, all alike in shape, size, and density, all stationary till struck. The administration wields the stick, sending rotund cue balls at students on the assumption that if the proper angle can be found, if students are struck in just the right spot, all will behave in proper fashion and inexorably be impelled in the ordained direction.

But the cue balls in this game are all different. A few students are smooth and well-rounded. Others are square or egg shaped, knobby or dented, flat or curvy. Some are ping-pong balls and some are bowling balls. Some look symmetrical, but inside weight is concentrated at peculiar places so they roll along in irregular and unpredictable fashion. Second, they are not stationary but in motion. They are not passive but in action. They are not clay for the potter, vessels to be filled, lamps to be lighted. The pool table is tipped and each ball is rolling. College experiences can accelerate, retard, or deflect the directions in which they move, depending upon the force and direction of the college experiences as they intersect with those of the student. But they have to connect with a moving target.

Until colleges and universities recognize the significance of individual differences much more explicitly and develop policies, practices, and educational resources accordingly, the promise of significant learning for the increasingly diverse kinds of students pursuing higher education will go unfulfilled. The place to begin is by conceptualizing more clearly some of the major dimensions of individual differences which need to be taken into account. They reside in three general areas: purposes and interests, skills and abilities, and cognitive styles.

The purposes and interests of college students today are causing many of the changes currently underway in the nation's colleges and universities. There is an aim to make it possible for students to create programs more finely tailored to their professional or vocational plans and aspirations, their social concerns, or their intellectual interests. These changes recognize that the opportunities for initial choice must be more complex, enabling new combinations of interdisciplinary study and new educational modes and processes. More important, colleges recognize that there must be opportunities for initial choices to be modified in response to new interests, new insights, and new questions that result from the learning itself. The more powerful the learning activities, the more likely it is that significant shifts in orientation and interest will occur. We can expect a student to continue along a singular direction at a constant rate only when the educational experiences are feeble or when they are irrelevant to his purposes or interests. Therefore, as education becomes more effective and more pertinent to matters significant for the students, we can expect to see demands for greater flexibility and individualization.

There is not much profit in detailing the wide array of interests and purposes that students bring to college and want to pursue while there. They typically fall in one or another of four general clusters or combinations of them: (1) Vocational/professional—expectations or requirements associated with various vocations, professions, certifying agencies, graduate schools, or other educational institutions. A prospective businessman, teacher, nurse, engineer, doctor, lawyer, psychologist, historian, or "other" will want to take these expectations and requirements into account. (2) Disciplinary/interdisciplinary—units and sequences associated with various traditional and emerging conceptions of the disciplines. A student who wants to develop thorough understanding and competence within one or more particular areas of knowledge can find useful guidelines and precedents by consulting various traditional arrangements or new interdisciplinary arrangements under development at other colleges and universities. (3) Problem oriented—knowledge and competence pertinent to various social problems and human concerns. A student who wants to tackle a social problem—population, environment, race, civil liberties, transportation, world peace—will need to obtain the knowledge and competence called for by his particular area of concern. (4) Avocational/practical—knowledge, competence, and experiences pertinent to various intellectual interests, recreational skills and activities, or immediately practical concerns. Most students will want to devote part of their energy to a variety of interests which are intrinsically satisfying or of direct practical value, but which do not necessarily serve the larger or more long range purposes mentioned above.

These varied purposes or interests share two characteristics: they are fairly easy to identify, and they are very susceptible to change. Given the right circumstances most students can identify their important interests and explain them with sufficient clarity for a faculty member to make sensible suggestions about appropriate areas of study and activities that connect most directly with the high points of the description as it is articulated at that time. The student can begin work. But the student and teacher must recognize that after some knowledge and perspective is acquired the formulations may be significantly altered, or that unexplored interests that looked tasty and nourishing may turn out to be flat and indigestible. The important thing is to develop educational arrangements which assist the original clarifications, which continue to assist when reformulation or major redefinition is called for, and which permit flexible program modifications in response to the changes that occur.

Skills and abilities of the college student are not as accessible to ready identification and definition as are his purposes and interests. Except in extreme instances, it takes time to determine what kinds of things a student can read with understanding and what kinds he cannot; it takes several papers and conferences to identify problems with sufficient precision to suggest helpful activities. More generalized levels of academic or intellectual competence, or motor and mechanical skill, are even more difficult to specify in ways that can be taken into account when students need help in planning programs and when an institution has to make decisions concerning educational materials and learning resources.

It is clear, for example, that there are wide ranging differences in scholastic aptitude. In 1962 McConnell and Heist reported scores on the American Council on Education Psychological Examination for 60,539 students in a sample of 200 schools. For individual institutions mean scores ranged from 36.5 to 142.2, a spread of nearly four standard deviations. The two extreme institutional means were equivalent to the first and ninety-second percentiles for the total population. That testing was before open admissions and before the new students from working class and disadvantaged backgrounds came on the scene in such large numbers. As more and more of these students enter colleges and universities, we can expect the range within each institution to approximate the range among institutions found by McConnell and Heist.

Furthermore, we recognize that the existing measures of scholastic aptitude miss many significant aspects of intellectual ability and working knowledge. They emphasize verbal skills and middle class information. The instruments for comprehensive and detailed assessment on which sound educational planning should be based simply are not in existence at this time. Bloom and his colleagues (1956) describe six dimensions of intellectual competence—knowledge, comprehension, application, analysis, synthesis, and evaluation—and give illustrative test items for each. But valid and reliable instruments with sound normative frameworks remain to be developed for these areas as well as for other conceptual frameworks which might prove equally helpful.

Yet, effective education depends upon effective management of the match between the skills and abilities of the student and the skills and abilities called for and thus fostered by the study activities and learning resources he is helped to pursue. The absence of sophisticated approaches to assess these areas does not mean we can ignore significant kinds of skills and abilities. It does mean, however, that we must operate on the basis of educated guesses and intuition, and that we must help students do the same, building in ample opportunities for self-correction as we see that our guesses have been off target.

There is a third dimension concurrent with the purposes and interests and the skills and abilities of college students that has been given considerable research attention during the past twenty years. This is the research on "cognitive styles" and personality characteristics related to these styles. These researchers have usually tried to restrict the meaning of "cognitive style" to modes of intellectual functioning which are consistent and pervasive within individuals, but which vary across types of individuals. It is difficult to operate within this tight definition, however, because one is taken quickly from cognition narrowly defined, to perception, and from perception to other significant variables that reflect consistent response patterns in social and interpersonal relationships. Therefore, especially in areas where substantial research has been undertaken, "cognitive style" turns out to be a very large umbrella.

There are other areas of style worth similar attention. There is research by Adorno and others (1950) on the authoritarian personality and Stern's findings (1962, 1967) concerning the differences in patterns of study and learning for "authoritarians," "antiauthoritarians," and "rationals." There are studies of dogmatism by Rokeach, and Barron's studies (1963) of belief systems. Research on creativity has been done by MacKinnon (1962), Heist (1968), and a host of others. Investigations of leveling and sharpening, constriction and flexibility, reflectiveness and impulsiveness, tolerance and intolerance for unrealistic experiences, analytical, relational and inferential differences, and automatization have been made by Broverman (1964), Gardner, Holzman, and others (1959); Gardner, Jackson and Messick (1960); Kagan, Moss, and Sigel (1963); Kagan, Rosman, and others (1964).

These fundamental dimensions of individual difference are

essential to take into account in developing educational resources and in individual program planning for the diverse students of today, be they residents or commuters. If we do not we will continue to miss the mark for substantial numbers of students.

The distinction between field-dependence and field-independence is one very useful conceptual framework for cognitive style, because it is clear and simple and has been elaborated by a rich array of diverse studies carried out over a twenty year period. The findings from these studies raise major questions for educational practice. They have been recently summarized in a paper entitled "The Role of Cognitive Style in Academic Performance and in Teacher-Student Relations" by Witkin (1972).

It all started with some simple rod and frame experiments. A person sits in a completely darkened room and faces a square frame painted with luminous paint within which is a rod similarly painted. Rod and frame can be tilted clockwise or counterclockwise independently. In a typical trial the person finds both rod and frame tilted and is asked to adjust the position of the rod so that it is upright. Both children and adults differ markedly in how they perform. In order to see the rod as upright some persons must align it with the frame. Even when the frame is tilted as much as thirty degrees to one side or another, they tilt the rod similarly but report that it is upright. At the other extreme, some persons bring the rod to a vertical position whatever the tilt of the frame.

Similar experiments use a chair and a small room, both of which can be tilted independently. The person starts seated in the chair with the room and the chair in tilted positions, and the task is to adjust his chair to an upright position. Some persons require that the chair be fully aligned with the surrounding room in order to perceive themselves upright. Even when they are tilted at a thirty degree angle, they report that they are perfectly straight, just as when they sit to eat dinner or in class. And again other persons bring themselves approximately upright regardless of the position of the room.

A third research situation involves the use of embedded pictures where a simple figure is contained in a complex field, like the puzzles found in many Sunday comics. Again there are marked differences in performance; for some persons the figure leaps into view, and others cannot find it even after prolonged search.

Various wrinkles on these fundamental methods have been used, but these suffice to indicate the operational definitions of field dependence and field independence. Individuals are highly consistent across the different methods. The continuum underlying individual differences in performance is the degree to which a person can deal with a part of the field separately from its surroundings, the extent to which he is able to dissemble items from an organized context, and the extent to which he has the capacity for perceptual analysis. Evidence accumulated since the first experiments demonstrates that the dimension of field dependence and field independence applies to problem solving behavior and to critical thinking as well as to perception. The research also indicates that this style extends into psychological domains beyond perception and cognition. The person who in the laboratory experiments is strongly influenced by the surrounding frameworks tends in social situations to use the prevailing frames of reference to define his attitudes, his beliefs, his feelings, and even his perceptions of himself. In developing attitudes toward various issues field-dependent persons are especially apt to adopt the positions held by an authority figure or by a peer group. In short, field dependence and field independence seem to be perceptual expressions of a broad range of personal functioning which extends into the realms of social and interpersonal behavior and into a wide range of other personality variables (Witkin and others, 1954; Witkin, 1965; Witkin and others 1962). These findings have been demonstrated for persons from diverse backgrounds within our own culture and for persons in other cultures—the Temne of Sierra Leone, the Eskimo of Baffin Bay, the Arunta of Australia, the Boat People and Hakka of Hong Kong.

Some of the findings particularly pertinent to curriculum planning, teaching, and learning are related to our present study.

Women and girls are more field-dependent than men and boys.

Field-independent students tend to choose vocations that call for analytical skills, such as the physical and biological sciences, mathematics, and engineering; field-dependent students avoid such domains and choose people-oriented work in teaching, counseling, selling, and supervisory positions in business.

Field-dependent students change majors more frequently,

and shifts out of mathematics and science are quite frequent whereas shifts out of the social sciences and humanities are relatively uncommon.

Field-independent teachers predominate in mathematics and the natural sciences, while teachers in the social sciences and humanities are more generally distributed across the full range from field dependence to field independence.

Field-dependent teachers prefer the discussion method of teaching; field-independent teachers prefer lecturing.

Field-independent teachers are more direct in their attempts to influence students; field-dependent teachers view democratic classroom procedures more favorably than field-independent teachers.

The performance of field-dependent students tends to be strongly affected by praise or criticism; field-independent students tend to be uninfluenced.

Teachers and students matched for field dependence or independence describe each other in highly positive terms, while teachers and students who are mismatched describe each other negatively; students viewed more positively not simply the personal characteristics but the intelligence and competence of teachers similar in cognitive style.

Field-independent persons more often use personal pronouns in their speech and use active verbs, saying "I do" for example, whereas field-dependent persons more often use transitive verbs, saying in effect, "things are done to me."

These findings have fundamental implications for educational practice. The basic difference between field-dependent and field-independent students lies in their analytic capacity, in their perceptual and cognitive ability to distinguish figure from ground, to separate a construct from its surrounding context and to restructure problem situations so that a construct can be used in a different way.

These differences amount to differences in the capacities required for those basic cycles of differentiation and integration on which learning and personal development depend. The field-dependent student, compared with his independent peer, needs stronger triggers if differentiation is to occur; a faculty member, fellow student, book, lecture, film, field experience, must present a greater degree of discontinuity, and must reveal it more obviously and powerfully, if it is to be perceived and acted on. Differentiation for the field-independent student, however, will be triggered much more readily. He may be blasted wide open by an experience that has little impact on his field-dependent classmate. Consequently, he may need to move much more quickly toward activities through which a higher level of integration may be achieved—quiet reflection, writing, long conversations with friends who are coping with similar issues. To be required to face a more extended and extensive barrage of stimuli may at the least be a waste of time, and at worst it may create serious problems. He may be faced with such a wide array of complex realizations that he is unable to get his head together before important decisions are required, or he may grasp too quickly and totalistically a new alternative that reduces anxiety and uncertainty, but that itself creates a new array of problems. We have seen both kinds of outcomes in our colleges and universities; students who have been untouched, and students who have been bowled over.

Effective education depends upon a sound match between the characteristics of the student and the characteristics of the programs and persons the student encounters, and the field-dependence-independence continuum represents a dimension of difference to take into account. It must also be taken into account for effective training, and all students need both training and education. The training program that is effective for the field-dependent student may not be for the independent student. Training usually involves an authoritarian dynamic and a working relationship with a supervising authority. This dynamic is much more likely to interfere with the successful achievement of the field-independent student than with his more dependent counterpart, and more often will need to be explicitly recognized and handled. The field-independent student will more frequently be distracted by questions of value, and, more frequently will want to know the whys and wherefores of various training requirements and procedures.

Research on cognitive styles has special pertinence to the major new higher education alternatives which, for the sake of parsimony, can be labeled "contract learning" and "programmed learning."

The varied approaches to contract learning usually share

three major characteristics. Programs are individually designed and implemented through conferences with a faculty member who is variously termed a mentor, advisor, preceptor, counselor. The emphasis is on building individualized educational programs which take each student's interests and purposes seriously, and which respond flexibly to those needs when they change. Often the programs can include field experiences as well as more typical academic activities such as readings, writing, specific courses, and the like.

The varied approaches to programed learning range all the way from highly articulated and systematized computer assisted instruction—which provides for complex branching on the basis of frequent examinations administered and corrected by the computer—through systematically organized printed materials, which include assigned readings accompanied by periodic papers and examinations that are sent to correspondence tutors for correction, to other more loosely organized study guides and reading lists that make little provision for systematic examination or feedback.

A bit of thought about the characteristics of field-dependent and field-independent students, and about the characteristics of field-dependent and -independent teachers, will suggest that neither of these new approaches is really on target. Both create double binds for students.

Take the field-dependent student first. The contract approach offers rich opportunities for human interaction. A student can actually sit down alone with a faculty member periodically and discuss his education at some length. Furthermore, he can build working relationships with other students and apprentice relationships with other adults into his educational program in ways that were not open to him before. The teaching approach is nonexpository, much closer to the discussion method than to lecturing. In these aspects it sounds ideal for the field-dependent student. It may be especially comfortable when he is working with a field-dependent teacher who is drawn to the contract approach primarily because of the opportunities for close human relationships it offers, and who lacks the tough analytic capacities of the field-independent teacher. But at the same time, the contract approach is highly self-referent. Students are asked to identify and clarify their own purposes and plans. They are asked to think about why they are going to college and what they want to accomplish by doing so. They are asked to take initiative for their own education, to say over and over, "I do," rather than "I am done to." But as the studies of communication patterns and much of the other research reported make clear, the capacity of the field-dependent student to be self-referent is limited. He finds it difficult to take himself, his own ideas, values, attitudes, plans, impulses, as the starting point for thinking and action. Given this double bind, it is not surprising that few field-dependent students, if I may now use the term loosely, have been found in the student-centered institutions and programs of the past, and that few are flocking in that direction today.

Programed learning presents a different set of problems for the field-dependent student. In programed learning the root assumption is that the student wants to learn what the program has to teach. Few programs really test that assumption. They may spell out the objectives so the student can make his choice on a reasonably informed basis, but then they simply start helping the student go to it. Programed learning, therefore, does not raise the self-referent questions posed by contract learning. But on the other hand, it is expository, it usually puts a premium on analytic skills, and it offers little or no opportunity for human interaction.

The field-independent student faces a different combination of problems. Contract learning suits very well his self-referent orientation and capacity to operate effectively without strong guidelines from authorities. He can tailor his level of study to his shifting levels of complexity and intensity and to his changing interests and purposes. But he may find it very difficult to obtain the challenges to his analytic skills that he needs to move through more complex and rapid cycles of differentiation and integration; and if he is not careful, his relative lack of social sensitivity may turn off his field-dependent faculty member. Programed learning is no answer for this student, because its authoritarian dynamic, its lack of flexibility, and its unresponsiveness to his strong desires to pursue particular interests and ideas to more complex and comprehensive levels, make it difficult for him to work at any single program very long. So there are still problems to be solved despite the promise of these new alternatives.

I would predict that carefully implemented studies of college dropouts and transfers would document these dynamics. I would hypothesize that the major reasons for the very high attrition rates for varied new alternatives that emphasize approaches analogous to programed learning—from the traditional correspondence courses to the British Open University—are essentially the same as those that account for the migration of students out of the biological and physical sciences into the humanities and social sciences. High proportions of field-dependent students leave the hard sciences, because those studies place a heavy emphasis on specific analytic skills and on independently derived conclusions based on those analyses. Human exchange and interaction is seldom a major concern. Field-dependent students move toward the social sciences and humanities because their strength in social sensitivity and their orientation toward human interaction are more appropriate to those studies and to the occupations that follow. Studies of dropouts and transfers from traditional institutions already document the case for the field-independent student. The dropouts consistently tend to be more autonomous, more complex, more impulsive, and less oriented toward practical achievement and materialistic success.

It will not be long before it will be possible to assess and to chart individual cognitive maps that characterize in rich, complex, and comprehensive ways, major modes of perceptual, cognitive, social, and interpersonal functioning. The contours of these maps will reflect major areas of individual strength and weakness and by so doing will allow each individual to conceptualize more clearly his own unique characteristics, and more importantly, these contours will provide guidelines by which each person can take more effective charge of his own education and personal development. Furthermore, increased awareness of these fundamental dimensions of individual difference can assist both students and teachers to make more sound judgements concerning future plans, aspirations, and the educational activities that are most likely to be productive for them.

## Differentiation and Integration

Education is essentially the amplification of two basic developmental processes—differentiation and integration. Increased differentiation occurs when one comes to see the interacting parts of some things formerly seen as unitary, when one distinguishes among concepts formerly seen as identical, when actions are more finely responsive to individual purposes or to outside conditions, when interests become more varied, tastes more diverse, reactions more subtle—in short, as we become complex human beings. It is to foster increased differentiation that a liberal arts college aims to free an individual from the limitations of outlook brought from his own locale, his family, his social class, and his national heritage—a freeing that may open the individual to all the possibilities and impossibilities of the world around him, a freeing that can lead to heightened sensitivity and awareness and that can also lead to coldness and insularity as the ways of the world are more clearly seen and more sharply experienced.

Increasing differentiation must be accompanied by increasing integration and this is the other major work of education. Relationships among parts must be perceived or constructed so more complex wholes result. Concepts from different disciplines must be brought to bear on one another and connected in ways appropriate to varied tasks or problems. Consistencies between word and word, word and deed, deed and deed must be achieved. Impulse and emotion must pull together with conscience and reason. Short run hedonism must coordinate with long run purposes. This formulation is basically that of Nevitt Sanford (1962, 1963, 1966). Helson's (1966) studies of adaptation levels and Pribram's (1967) writing on "The New Neurology and the Biology of Emotion: a Structural Approach" also are pertinent.

The process of differentiation and integration are often accompanied by concurrent cycles of disequilibrium and equilibrium. When we see things we have not seen before or run into new experiences for which our past has not prepared us, we may be knocked off balance. Sometimes when we get leaned on this way we can snap back to our original position when the pressure goes away. On other occasions, if we are pushed hard enough, we have to move our feet, to shift to another position. To be educable, therefore, means to be open to such temporary periods of disorganization and disequilibrium, in the confidence that one will be able to recover and that the new position discovered as a consequence will provide a more sound foundation for further movement in response to additional challenges.

Helson's numerous studies of adaptation levels document this process clearly. He says, "We must distinguish between the *physical* stimulus and the *effective* stimulus. . . . The effective stimulus depends upon the state of the organism, upon preceding and accompanying stimuli, and, in some cases, upon possible future outcomes of stimulation. . . . Most of the difficulties of stimulus theories of motivation vanish if we take as the zero of intensity not the absolute threshold [the level at which a stimulus barely can be perceived] but the adaptation level. It then follows that stimuli below the level as well as above the level may possess motivating power because it is discrepancy from level in either direction that determines affective quality and its distinctiveness" (1966, pp. 144, 147).

Differentiation and integration then, are useful ways to think about the educational process. Whether or not differentiation occurs depends on the match between the expectations, adaptations, and purposes established on the basis of past experiences and the intensity and configuration of new experiences. Detailed case histories would reveal the significant areas of match and mismatch between the backgrounds of commuters and residents and the college environments and experiences they encountered. We would then see substantial differences in patterns of differentiation and integration which could help us understand more clearly the significant variables and dynamics that underlie the differences in educational outcomes.

Recommendations for action to improve the quality of higher education for commuting students should take account of these general conceptual frameworks. They should amplify the processes of differentiation and integration that are at work for commuters as well as residents. They should provide arrangements so that individual differences in interests and purposes, in skills and abilities, and in cognitive styles can be recognized by students and faculty members. They should suggest ways in which the powerful forces generated by interpersonal relationships and group membership can be made more readily available.

Educational effectiveness for the new students entering higher education—most of whom are commuters whose contact with faculty members, other students, and the institution is limited—will depend heavily on our capacity to create the administrative processes, the educational arrangements, and the faculty members which will help implement new alternatives and help each student choose those most effective for him. With institutional development of this kind, we can improve the fit between each student and his college. If such development is not undertaken, increasing numbers of students will continue to quit and to wander from program to program, school to school, seeking, in trial and error fashion, a setting where their own learning and personal development will go forward.

# 9

# *Recommendations*

$E$ffective education depends fundamentally on a sound match between the educational needs and purposes of the student, the curricular alternatives and learning resources made available to him through an efficient use of human and material resources, and on the educational power of these alternatives and resources. Commuters find it especially difficult to achieve this match solely on the basis of their own initiative because of their psychological, social, and physical distance from the college; institutional assistance can be critically important to them. Resident students can use such assistance as well, but their presence on campus, their easy access to pertinent information and to the grapevines that carry it, make it more possible for them to find educational programs and experiences that suit their interests and abilities. The recommendations which follow, therefore, have special potential for commuters, but they will increase institutional effectiveness for the resident students as well.

These recommendations call for new arrangements in three major areas. The first includes activities by which students get started, plan their program, monitor their progress, and make whatever changes are called for as they move along—admissions, orientation, program planning, and program review. The second area includes teaching, curriculum, and the varied learning resources—field experiences, programed learning materials, special instruction. The third concerns new approaches to residential experiences which aim both to amplify the educational power of those experiences and to make them more widely accessible and more economically feasible for commuting students and the institutions that serve them.

### Orientation and Admissions

All students moving toward higher education need information about the system and about the institution they aim to attend, information about how it operates and how they can use it to best advantage. These needs are especially strong in the new students from working class homes and from disadvantaged backgrounds where few parents and fewer older friends have attended college. Knoell (1968) spells out the problem:

> Community colleges are by nature open-door institutions—free to those who cannot afford the low tuition and fees, comprehensive in curricular offerings, located close to population centers, and responsive to local needs for education beyond high school. Yet, in the name of administrative expediency, procedural barriers are often erected—subtly discriminatory barriers which may have the effect of rendering the colleges inaccessible to the poor, the educationally handicapped, and others lacking the necessary 'savy' to cope with a bureaucratic system.

Many admission procedures, application instructions, and financial aid forms are challenging for the experienced college-educated parents and for their offspring. About two years ago I sat down to read the booklet of general instructions for applying to one or another of the colleges and universities of the State University of New York. I read it through once, then again, and then again. Even after the third reading—and after forty-five years of education, international travel, three degrees, and twelve years of direct experience in higher education—there were things I was not sure I understood. The State University of New York (SUNY) now serves more than 350,000 students so it is obvious that somehow they get in, and probably that booklet helps. But it certainly is not easy reading. I also helped design the admissions application for Empire State College, a new institution which aims to serve a wide range of different kinds of students. Because of the special nature of the institution and the demands implicit in its program, we ask students to answer some basic questions which some of them have never thought much about before. "What kind of life do you want to be leading five or ten years from now? What is apt to be your family situation? What kind of community might you be living in? What are your long range vocational or professional plans or aspirations? What kinds of work do you want to be doing five or ten years from now? What are your current responsibilities and obligations? Which of these will continue as you pursue your program at Empire State? With which Learning Center will you affiliate? What resources for learning does it offer which seem useful to you? Are there persons, places, instructional materials, or other resources that you may wish to use in addition to those available through the Center? How might you begin your studies? What resources might you use? What sequence of activities might you undertake?"

To increase the chance that these questions receive serious thought, we ask students to answer them as part of their application. The questions are not in the service of administrative expedience, indeed they make our lives more complicated than if we ignored them. The questions present problems for many of our potential enrollees who have limited verbal skills, who are embarrassed by their limitations, and who have never reflected seriously about themselves and their future, or about education in these terms.

The point is not that such questions should be set aside, or that SUNY should not request the data, or that judgements about financial aid should rest on more minimal information. I think the questions asked by Empire State serve valid educational purposes, and I think the other information requested in the admissions' brochure also serves useful purposes. However, many students need help right at the beginning, before they are ever admitted. If that help is not available, many will not find their way to the educational experiences they need.

Admission to college therefore, especially for commuting students, starts with preadmission information and assistance. Empire

State's program and experience are relevent here. Each institution needs to develop admission and orientation centers where students can obtain the help they need to decide whether to apply, to manage the necessary procedures, and to begin thinking about what they will actually do after they are admitted. This center is supplied with diverse materials that give potential students basic information. There are descriptions of program alternatives, examples of what students with different educational objectives actually do; information about the interests and backgrounds of faculty members, about community resources, volunteer activities, and work study alternatives that can be built into academic programs. A tape-slide show presents information about the program to supplement these other materials.

The center is staffed by persons who can answer questions raised by these materials. The most helpful staff members are older students who receive compensation from work-study monies or other financial aid, who know the ropes, and who can give concrete and direct information out of their own experiences. If the prospective student or the staff member does not have the time for an individual conference, the student is informed of group meetings scheduled during the day and during the evening. The emphasis in these group meetings is on answering questions, not on delivering basic information.

Time invested in group meetings is generally better spent than in individual conferences. In two hours thirty students cover a lot of territory, and much of it will be useful for most of them. Many questions will be discussed that never occur to a student sitting alone. Many possibilities for areas he might study, resources he might use, approaches he might take, which he would not have thought possible, will be suggested. This experience helps him think more precisely about why he wants to go to college and why to this college; about what he will do when he has enrolled. It also helps him decide not to enroll and to pursue other alternatives that may be more appropriate if it really looks as though his purposes cannot be well served.

Although it is not a requirement, students are urged to examine the materials available and to attend sessions at the center where information and help is available before actually applying. When completed applications have been received the admissions' decision rests primarily on judgements concerning the capacity of the institution to respond to the educational needs and purposes of the student. If the institution does not have the necessary capacity, if it lacks the competence on the faculty, if it lacks critical facilities or other resources and has no access to them, it must be candid about its limitations. If possible, the reply to the applicant should indicate other institutions or programs that can meet his needs. When an institution has the appropriate resources, and when space is available, the student is accepted and assigned to an orientation workshop.

Assignments to workshops are primarily based on the future plans and educational interests the student has indicated on his application, and efforts are made to bring students with similar interests together. However, it is sound to have, as well, students with diverse backgrounds and interests. The orientation workshop aims to serve four major purposes for individual students: to help him think through more explicitly his purposes and the educational program he wants to pursue; to help him become better acquainted with the institutional resources—faculty members, courses, instructional materials, field experiences—he may want to use and decide where he should begin; to introduce him to other students with whom he might work; to provide an explicit point of departure from which to build an identification with the institution and with some of the persons who are part of it. Because these elements are critical to an effective beginning, all students are asked to attend an orientation workshop before making the enrollment commitment required by a tuition payment, and because it has substantial educational value for the student even if he decides not to enroll. At Empire State a fee is charged which provides income sufficient to cover basic costs (thirty dollars in 1973). The workshop ideally runs about two and one half days and deals with forty to fifty students. Simple overnight accomodations are available, meals are provided without extra charge, and students are urged to stay from beginning to end. Selected faculty members also participate through the full workshop period.

The workshop begins with a brief welcoming statement and moves quickly into a series of small group meetings which bring together different combinations of background and interest of students and faculty members. In these groups students describe their general plans and educational interests and one or two faculty members do likewise. Each session lasts an hour or two, and after three rounds of meetings each student has been exposed to most others in attendance. He also has described his own plans two or three times, and it is interesting to observe the changes that occur in the descriptions. These meetings may be interrupted by, or followed by, opportunities for informal conversation at a meal, a social hour, or by some free late evening time.

The workshop next turns to small group meetings based on generally defined areas of student interest. In these meetings one or two older students describe their own programs and those of others they know, and with the help of faculty members they answer questions about varied alternatives which students may want to pursue. These meetings last two or three hours, and students are urged to attend a full session, even though they may be torn between different interest areas.

The workshop provides substantial time for individual conferences with an older student or with a faculty member. Scheduling problems can be difficult. Although conferences may be limited to thirty minutes, students may still have to wait. All educational materials about program alternatives and the college should be available for students to read while waiting for appointments. This also is a time when students can complete questionnaires, interest inventories, achievement tests, or other information gathering instruments needed for institutional research and planning.

The workshop schedules a formal though brief final general session, often held during or at the end of a final meal. This is a more successful technique than leaving students to peter out after their individual conferences.

An effective orientation workshop will have different outcomes for different students. Some students become aware of possibilities they never thought of pursuing before. Other students see how to put together combinations of interests, abilities, and future aspirations that had seemed irreconcilable. Some students recognize particular areas of competence or knowledge that need direct attention; others discover ways to begin despite shortcomings. A few may become more conscious of their own styles and how they can work best in more general terms. A small proportion may begin to identify with others who are also entering, with already enrolled students, or with the institution itself. Some students decide that the college is not for them and do not follow through with tuition payment; others formulate a clear educational program that they can pursue with energy and interest. In most cases these diverse outcomes are positive and productive. The student who enrolls gets off to a more sound start, and the student who does not moves more expeditiously and more knowledgeably to other alternatives.

A small group of students will emerge from the orientation workshop who want to enroll but who need various kinds of follow up, either before enrolling or afterward. Some may want to obtain special instruction in reading or writing. Some may want to explore particular interests or employment aspirations in detail. Some may want to test their capacities for independent study. These students may make explicit plans which in effect extend their orientation period. Sometimes the activities can be planned as part of their academic program and carried on within the regular tuition and fee structure. On other occasions it makes sense for them to be carried on outside of that structure under special arrangements made by the institution or by the student himself. The orientation workshop, therefore, really is the beginning of an orienting process which the student continues with varying degrees of self-consciousness throughout his career. The workshops can take place at other periods as well.

The orientation workshop outlined above is based on our experiences at Empire State College. We have tried many different combinations, and, although further experimentation could be constructive, I think this pattern best accomplishes the four major purposes for which it is designed.

Certain problems are inherent in the workshops described above. Not all students will be able to stay overnight. Not all will want to take the time for full and uninterrupted participation. Exceptions have to be made. Some students and faculty will think there should be no fee, or the fee is too high. In my own judgement, the fee is valuable, as it testifies to the significance of the workshop and helps strengthen the students' commitment to full participation.

Some faculty members will not want to participate. Administratively, it is an added burden. Faculty often do not see it as part of their role or responsibility; they think it should be handled by counselors, student personnel staff members, or others. My own view is that faculty participation is critical. There is little that more effectively helps a student get started, identify with the institution, or meet problems throughout his college years, than a personal acquaintance with a faculty member. Moore indicates the fundamental reason: "Above all other things, disadvantaged students know that there is little dialogue between themselves and higher education as a whole. Most of them are convinced that when they talk to college personnel, the college people are not listening. They are convinced that people in higher education neither really know about their problems specifically nor understand them generally. They believe it is only a matter of time before the selection process of the community college becomes, as it is in the university level, a process to eliminate the vast majority of the poor. In short, disadvantaged students do not feel that the community college really gives a damn" (1970, pp. 59, 60). Moore's comments focus on the disadvantaged, but our findings concerning commuting students in general, and research on resident students as well (Chickering, 1970, for example), indicate that limited communication and exchange with faculty is not restricted to disadvantaged students or to the community colleges. Initial contact is especially important for commuters who need to build strong bridges to the college.

The face to face contact with these students can be even more important for the faculty members. Participation keeps faculty in touch with students and their backgrounds. They see the students fresh before collegiate styles are superficially acquired. Faculty participation, therefore, can undercut in a direct way the basis for student assertions concerning faculty naivete and lack of interest.

Given the problems, it is easy to find reasons for not undertaking orientation workshops. But for commuting students, and especially for new students from disadvantaged backgrounds and from working class families, the promises far outweigh the problems. As educational options multiply so do the opportunities for sound choices and effective matchmaking between student needs and educational resources, or the opportunity for error. Therefore, as the opportunities multiply procedures for admission and orientation become increasingly important.

## Program Planning and Review

The initial orientation activities are not the end of educational planning. Educational planning continues through college, and for more and more persons it continues periodically after an undergraduate degree has been obtained. The process is strengthened if explicit plans are periodically formulated even though they may be held with only tenuous tenacity. Most students can set forth only short term predictions in the orientation workshops, which must depend upon additional knowledge and experience before they can be spelled out further. Most beginning students want to explore, to test the water, even when they are quite firmly convinced of what they want to do.

Before too long, however, a student needs to lay out a reasonably detailed program of study that describes his major areas of effort and ties these to a rough time table. These plans for what is called his "concentration area" are not cast in concrete. They can be changed when there are good reasons to do so. The need to design an area of concentration provides a framework in which the student thinks about his educational plans in some detail, in the light of his past experiences and his future plans. Planning thereafter is less frequently ad hoc and more frequently in the context of the broader perspective that the program of study has provided.

At Empire State, when the student judges himself close to the completion of his program he submits a record of the major kinds of work he has satisfactorily completed and a statement of his future plans, including any formal educational activities, to a faculty committee. If this committee agrees that his program has been satisfactorily completed they recommend him for graduation; if they do not, they indicate the additional needed areas of work. In recommending graduation, the committee may also make suggestions concerning the person's future plans if it seems useful.

The basic assumptions which underlie these recommendations for admissions, orientation, program planning and review have been clearly given. Students themselves and the institutions which serve them need to be more self-conscious and more explicit about the educational processes and programs in which they invest their time and energy. This self-consciousness and explicitness is required because, in the face of multiple alternatives, there are significant individual differences among students, which all the pressures of daily routines, administrative procedures, large numbers, limited resources, and flying time work to obscure, to minimize, and to actively disregard. These forces work against the institutions and the students, and they are heightened for the commuting students. Only by continually working against such forces can the significant dimensions of individual difference be kept in sight so that sound matching can achieve effective and efficient education.

### Curriculum

The educational needs and styles of the diverse students entering each two- and four-year college and university must be met with an equally diverse array of curricular alternatives, learning resources, and teaching practices. Furthermore, these elements must be systematically linked. To consider one element in isolation from the others is unwise, to change one part without threatening the others is almost impossible. Each element, however, can be discussed individually.

In the late sixties I visited a predominantly black southern college whose primary concern was a very high attrition rate. The students came mainly from rural and poor southern families. What was the required curriculum for those students who went to their first classes full of anxiety and uncertainty? History of Western civilization, English composition, introductory biology or introductory chemistry, music appreciation, English literature. There was no novel by a black novelist, no poetry by a black poet. The music appreciation course never touched jazz or mentioned a black musician. The history of Western civilization course never came within a hundred years of slavery and the plantation culture of the south. The defense of these requirements was that these students needed to become "well-rounded" and liberally educated. Now there was certainly no question about that need. The only problem was that not many students were ready for this challenge; not many stayed to meet it. Eighty percent of the freshmen were gone by summer. Man, they didn't want to become well-rounded. They wanted help in getting better jobs and more money, and in the basic skills that would let them do so. With these in hand there might be something to be well-rounded about, there might be some reason to reach for something more. They could have moved directly into studies relevant to their professional or vocational interests; or if they had a shot at some of the courses being offered by the Vermont Community Colleges for their rural disadvantaged students— "How to be Poor and Survive in the Seventies," "Comparative Shopping and Buying on Credit," "Basic Home Maintenance and Appliance Repair"—they might have stayed on for more general studies and might have developed the motivation to pursue them.

In recognizing the crucial importance of individual differences and of devising relevant curriculum, we are not ignoring the significance of "the structure of the disciplines." Some sequences and patterns of organization are more logical, easier to communicate, and easier to grasp than others. In some areas—fewer than we thought ten years ago—certain skills and knowledge must be acquired before additional levels of understanding and competence can be pursued. Of course, there is widespread variation and debate on what a "discipline" is and how it should be studied. For some biologists, for example, biology concerns what goes on inside the skin; they study organ functioning, relationships among organs and their contributions to the whole. Other biologists see the organism as just half of a transactional relationship with the environment. For them biology concerns the homeostatic processes through which equilibrium is maintained. The research methods, the relevant evidence, the central concepts and information differ depending upon which kind of biologist you are. And within each of these general orientations particular sequences and emphases vary.

Few disciplines have a universally agreed upon structure. Debates concerning the value of one approach over another are valuable. To argue for relevance and recognition of individual differences is not to suggest that these considerations be ignored.

Instead it makes the problems more complicated, for it suggests that disciplinary structures themselves must vary depending upon student characteristics.

The familiar dichotomy of content and process is one useful way to tackle the problem of relevance. Some content—information, concepts, ideas, insights, fantasies, experiences direct and vicarious— can relate to the past content, problems, and concerns of students quite directly, while other content can not. Most of the conceptions of self and world and most of the behavioral norms and standards that students bring to college have been adopted rather uncritically from parents, community, and friends. Study of history, religion, anthropology, sociology, and economics, as well as psychology, philosophy, and literature can challenge these conceptions and behaviors and can broaden the perspective within which they are held and acted upon.

Katz and Sanford observed the challenge of relevance at work in their studies at Vassar and Stanford. "The student's natural inclination, of course, is to judge characters in literature, as well as elsewhere, according to the values he brings with him to college. . . . But if he gets the point, if he discovers that anything can be done in the imagination and that everything he has so far imagined has been done by somebody and that those who did these things can be understood, then he is bound to admit into his scheme of things a broader range of human potentialities. These he can see as present in himself as well as in other people" (1962, pp. 439, 440).

Study in the natural sciences can raise powerful and fundamental questions of concern to all of us. The Scopes trial was neither the first nor the last occasion when scientific theory and research challenged fundamental belief systems and value frameworks. When Copernicus took man and earth from the center and sent them spinning around the sun he also sent some basic beliefs into orbit. Nobel's dynamite, a lady-finger firecracker in today's perspective, raised moral questions currently reconfronted in decisions concerning nuclear warfare. Mathematics teaches that initial assumptions can define a system which solves some problems and not others and that several different systems may solve the same problem. Einstein's relativity theories, quantum theory, other more recent discoveries concerning genetic control, new techniques for organ transplants, improved techniques for keeping the infirm and elderly alive—all these raise similar fundamental issues concerning life, death, time, space, social responsibility.

Fancy laboratories and expensive equipment are not required; recognition of where students are and a bit of creative thought can teach basic concepts while speaking to fundamental concerns. Ted Merrill, who teaches biology at Goddard College, an institution not renowned for its wealth or elaborate plant, has shared a good example of what I mean. He obtains fertile eggs from a local chicken house and has his students crack them open and examine them. The first eggs opened are a day or so old, the next two days, the next three, four, five, and so on. As each new series of eggs are cracked open the development of the chicken becomes more and more apparent. Blood becomes evident, the body begins to take shape, the beating heart becomes observable. As these changes in the eggs are observed, changes also start to take place in the students and in their reactions and orientations. What was simply an academic and scientific exercise takes on significant human and value dimensions. Many students become more and more hesitant to continue, some refuse to go on as the lives they are taking become ever more obvious. Discussions of basic biological and genetic concepts and readings in these areas are increasingly interrupted by or interspersed with discussion and readings concerning abortion, population control, genetic manipulation, high altitude bombing and other forms of killing at a distance.

This is but a single small unit, occupying not more than a week or two. But the biology lessons learned are not forgotten, and eggs for breakfast keep the existential issues alive for months afterward.

Studies that speak to basic existential questions and to the immediate issues of autonomy and identity, of emotional awareness and control, of interpersonal relationships and integrity, not only help identify the basic concepts and knowledge of the particular discipline pursued, but also help students make progress in the areas of personal development which are important to them.

Contemporary social problems bear equal attention in creating relevant content in the curriculum. Benezet (*Chronicle of*

*Higher Education,* November 20, 1972, p. 8) has written on this
point.

> The cry of the student for attention to the con-
> temporary problems of life cannot be disregarded as the
> numbers of people going to college continue to rise. Few
> of the eight and one half million now attending college
> will become professional scholars. Almost all will become
> citizens, voters, family heads, world neighbors, and, to
> varying degrees, leaders of opinion.
>
> The modern university should re-examine the con-
> tent and meaning of its program leading to the bachelor
> of arts. Environmental study of the closed bio-system
> which is spaceship Earth should become one basic element
> in the curriculum. Human identity revealed in the differ-
> ent races and cultures at home and abroad, often at con-
> flict with each other, should be a second. The political
> economy of a nation tied to the political economy of the
> rest of the world should be a third. The forms and vari-
> eties of creative leisure, applying the humanities and the
> arts toward preserving human individuality should be a
> fourth.
>
> The students are ready and eager for curriculum
> developments involving these elements. Their inability to
> find enough of them in the existing curriculum helps turn
> them off into preoccupations with sex, drugs, occultism
> (including a revival of witchcraft), and a general rejec-
> tion of rationalism or of the record of past intellectual
> accomplishment.

Curricular arrangements such as these referred to above are
of particular importance to the new students who are coming from
the middle and upper middle class communities from which most
college students have traditionally come. The new students from
working class homes and from disadvantaged backgrounds also
share these concerns; it is a mistake to think they do not. But their
priorities often have to be different. They are especially tuned to
immediate results rather than to long range expectations and delayed gratifications. Too many broken promises, too many hopes
turned to dust have drained the motivation from tasks whose out-

comes are far distant. In many cases the immediate demands of reality for bread and bed, for clothes and books, do not leave much time for the explorations, perigrinations, and shifting orientations of their more affluent peers.

Fantini and Weinstein point out, "career-oriented education is really the most humanistic education if we acknowledge that education in a free society should enable an individual to pursue . . . satisfying careers in the world of work, as a parent, and as a citizen, to sense that he is something of value, that he is growing positively, and that he is cultivating—and being helped by society to cultivate— his potential" (1968). Colleges that attract students with strong professional interests can capitalize on them. Professional and vocational preparation can be more than training students to use narrowly defined concepts, skills, and terminology. Students can place their plans for work in the context of the life styles of persons up-the-line from where they will enter to find out how they got there and what the more advanced positions require. By modifying the processes, content, and direct experiences which are built into professional and vocational education, many significant dimensions of educational and personal development can be amplified and accelerated. The "upside down curriculum" which begins by giving primary attention to vocational or professional preparation and delays general studies recognizes these basic notions.

Up to this point the discussion of relevance has focused on content more than process. At all levels of education, and especially in higher education, there has been more thought given to what should be learned and to how different constellations of subject matters are appropriately defined, than to different styles and processes by which learning occurs.

The evidence on individual differences in aptitudes and the research on cognitive styles and on other personality dispositions has demonstrated, however, that there are significant differences in how persons learn and that these differences interact with particular areas of content and competence. We need to know much more about how such processes influence the learning of anthropology, calculus, history, sociology, secretarial practice, literature, nursing, physics, teaching, and all the areas of content and competence that students want to take unto themselves. Without that knowledge we have to rely on our own crude guesses concerning the amount of structure or freedom most appropriate for a given student, or the degree to which he needs to learn from concrete experiences and to go from there to abstract generalizations. The experiences provided by attempting such guesses, acting on them, and observing the outcomes may help us improve. Furthermore they may provide the soil which can nourish more systematic studies to supplement our intuitions.

Relevant content and relevant processes become much more possible when direct experiences are part of the academic program. On-the-job experiences and apprentice relationships, volunteer activities, travel, field studies, and observations add a dimension which can convert abstract concepts into working knowledge and which can provide hitching posts for further conceptualizations. Bower (1966, pp. 121, 131, 132) has emphasized this point:

> It is important for schools to provide real events, objects, and relationships to which symbols can be tied. "Democracy" or "freedom," as words, are meaningless and their use dangerous unless a child learns them in a context of doing and thinking. This is especially true of symbols with high-level abstract meaning. Such symbols, unless tied down by first-hand experiences, are like boats in a storm, to be tossed this way and that, depending on the wind or current. . . . If objects are not bound into symbols by action, they tend to remain unintegrated and fragmented. Bergson suggested that, in some men, perceiving and acting are separate entities. When such persons look at a thing, "they see it for itself and not for themselves." These are people who are born with or have developed a detachment from life. This is a reminder of the Swiss gentleman who, when given a choice between going to paradise or going to a lecture about paradise, chose the latter.

Until very recently print has reigned unchallenged; higher education is still basically hooked on books. Yet most things are learned more fully and more permanently otherwise. Curricular changes that permit commuting students to take advantage of their work and living situations will add both power and relevance to their education. It also will help them build more effectively on the concrete knowledge they already have, to convert the teachings of their peers and the streets into larger meanings, to associate those experiences with more general conceptual frameworks, adding meaning both to the experiences themselves and to the basic concepts to be grasped.

If these principles are followed, the curriculum for each student becomes what he does to learn what he needs to learn and to develop the competence he needs to acquire, to pursue the purposes and interests of primary importance to him during his college career. The curriculum of an institution no longer exists in the abstract, without reference to a particular person. The educational program becomes the aggregate of these individual programs of study and the patterns by which they are implemented. Generalizations can be abstracted from the programs and patterns which different students develop, but behind these generalizations no two programs are exactly alike. Individual examples can be created to illustrate how students tend to work in different areas, but no example can simply be multiplied by 100 and thereby codified for all students of a given class.

The emphasis on creating individual curricula that reflect individual interests, abilities, and learning styles may suggest a laissez faire attitude. There is no doubt about that danger. That is why orientation and explicit program planning and review must be emphasized. Unless tough minded implementation by the faculty as a collegial unit and by individual faculty members as they work directly with students accompanies individualization, we will simply have shifted from the totalism of detailed requirements to a totalism that ignores the realities of professional competence and personal development. But this tough mindedness becomes more difficult as at the same time we venture toward the use of new and diverse kinds of experiences and resources which students can legitimately build into their programs.

## Learning Resources

If each person is to be effectively matched with curricular alternatives relevant to his interests and aspirations, to his skill, abilities, and cognitive style, a wide range of resources must be available. If the range is limited, then the programs of study also will be limited. Therefore, increasing recognition of significant individual differences must be accompanied by an expanded range of resources.

Commuting students have the courses, the laboratory, and the library available to them. But as our findings make clear, commuting students do not make use of these resources as effectively as their residential peers. The classes and instructors they might particularly like to work with may be scheduled at times that conflict with work and family obligations. Friends and reference groups in their home communities cut into the time and energy available to establish new relationships and to connect effectively with these on-campus resources for learning. They need specialized information and assistance to help them identify and make use of other persons and experiences pertinent to their educational purposes.

Despite dramatic advances in technology, human resources remain the cornerstone of significant education. These human resources include not only faculty members and professional persons outside the academic realm, but also other students. If an individual student is to capitalize on these rich resource persons, he or she needs to know who they are, where they are, and what they can and will contribute. Basic directories, which are relatively simple to develop and maintain, can make this human talent and other resources accessible to the commuting student. These directories can also expand the alternatives which resident students know of and can use. The directory should include, for those students who are willing, basic information such as name, address, and telephone number, accompanied by additional information such as major areas of intellectual interest and academic study, major recreational activities or interests, professional-vocational or avocational pursuits, and special skills or competence a student is willing to share for free or for a price. This information should be organized by last name alphabetically, by subheadings within each of the first four categories above, and by geographical location. With this directory a student can look up another individual whose name may have been mentioned to him, or he can identify an array of individuals who share particular intellectual-academic, professional-vocational, or avocational-recreational interests. The commuter could also identify students within his local calling area or within an easy drive. This student directory can be a direct resource for students and faculty as they plan programs of study or as they develop short-term seminars, weekend workshops, or other group efforts. The directory can also help a student identify another individual with whom he or she might work cooperatively or in a shared teaching-learning relationship.

A similar directory can be prepared for faculty members, tutors, field supervisors, and other resource persons on whom a student might want to call. This directory indicates not only the resource person's major fields or professional competences, but also other areas of intellectual or avocational interests and experiences. For tutors and field supervisors it indicates the ways in which they work with students, the resources they can supply or provide access to, and the usual costs.

A directory of other institutions and organizations in the community can help a student identify those most pertinent to his program. Such a directory, being developed at Empire State College, is organized in seven major categories: business/industry, cultural organizations, educational institutions, environmental organizations, governmental agencies, museums, social agencies. The name, address, and telephone number of each organization is given together with information concerning contact persons, and a brief description of the educational resources available.

Listings must be selected and continually evaluated for the effectiveness with which students use the resources. A huge list comparable to the Manhattan Yellow Pages is not necessary, and, moreover, because of the sheer volume, it is disfunctional. It is much better to have a small array of high-quality alternatives within each major area of student interest. Quality depends on evidence demonstrating the educational value of the activities students pursue, on the adequacy of supervision students receive, and on the soundness of the evaluation of his performance and of his learning which is provided either by persons in the institution with whom the student works or by a field supervisor who monitors students' performance in several such settings. The directory should include available resources for sports and recreational activities. It should include a section on

personal services. Although the college itself need not necessarily
provide such things as medical services or psychological counseling,
it can maintain up-to-date lists of doctors, clinics, emergency rooms,
psychotherapists, psychiatrists, and a wide range of voluntary organizations, which students can call on for assistance. With these student, faculty, and community directories available, each student can
begin to take effective charge of his own education, and each faculty
member can expand his reach beyond the texts and journals with
which he is familiar.

### Programed Learning

The human and community resources suggested above can
be powerfully amplified by varied kinds of systematically organized
study guides and programed learning materials. But these materials
need to become more varied in format, complexity, and comprehen-
siveness than has been the case in the past. Most programed learning
materials aim toward a relatively singular outcome or specific
objective. They can be relatively broad in scope, but everyone is
supposed to start at about the same level of ability and knowledge
and end with the same level of competence or understanding. Most
programs are like a fat diamond. The starting point is narrow and
so is the end, while in the middle there is a network of interlocking
branches that students follow depending upon their particular
successes and failures and particular areas of special interest or
ability. The typical programed learning materials can do an effective
job for certain purposes, but another quite different approach is
needed. This approach must create materials that look much more
like a forest. Each program provides a different starting place and
leads to sets of branches that become farther and farther apart as a
student moves higher and higher. The programs are sufficiently
interrelated so that the branches of one overlap with the branches
of others. Then a student can either go straight through the program
pursuing a singular line of inquiry or expertise or range around
through various levels and areas of knowledge or competence. The
programs can help students draw on the varied human and other
resources of the communities and suggest how these resources can
be used. The programs can be specifically designed combinations of

activities which help a student achieve a specific kind of competence or understanding for delineated purposes. The program can start with elementary work and proceed through greater levels of complexity and sophistication so that advanced students also will find useful entry points. Each program identifies points of contact with other programs in the same discipline or in other related areas. These programs need not be conceived as courses. They are a larger unit interrelated to a wide range of alternatives which can be assembled around a common method, theme, or particular student interest or purpose. In consultation with a faculty member, or on his own if he has the competence, a student can then assemble his own curriculum using materials from many different areas in ways that make sense to his purposes and background.

Each student does not have to work alone or in isolation. Appropriate points for contact with faculty members and other resource persons are suggested. Some programs begin with brief one- or two-day seminars which introduce several students at once to the work to be undertaken. Others may call for periodic residential workshops.

Faculty members make use of these program materials in several ways. For one student it may be desirable to build an entire area of concentration around a series of materials outlined by the program developers. Another student may use discrete aspects of a number of different program plans which call for independent readings and field experiences identified by the faculty member and student.

The basic point is that our conceptions concerning programed learning need to move beyond the typical pattern of sharply defined objectives and clearly articulated paths to those objectives. There will be continued need for a wide range of programed materials of that kind, but there is also a great need for a different approach which is much more open ended. It gives a student diverse suggestions that are systematically related and that include not only readings, films, and audio materials, but also recommendations for field experiences, resource persons, and faculty consultation. With these materials available each student then has guidance in building study plans appropriate for him. At the same time the range of resources available to each faculty member is increased, and his range of competence becomes more extensive as he has the benefit of these varied suggestions and observes the programatic relationships.

## Teaching

If an institution develops a curricular orientation that recognizes the significance of individual differences, and if it develops an array of learning resources commensurate with the diverse kinds of students to be served, it needs one more key ingredient. This ingredient is in scarce supply on most campuses, but it can be cultivated and can flourish.

This master teacher carries multiple responsibilities quite different from those of the typical teacher of the past. He does not only know a particular field well, but also has broad information and interests. He can listen and respond with understanding to a student's plans and aspirations, his fears and anxieties, and his uncertain ideas about what to do and how to proceed. The master teacher analyzes the student's strengths and weaknesses, he helps him identify his past accomplishments and their relationships to his future plans so that the areas of study necessary to reach his goals can be more clearly specified. Often he makes suggestions, helping the student develop independent studies and helping him connect with teachers, tutors, and field supervisors whose special talents suit the student's needs. In these activities the master teacher becomes an educational leader for the other resource persons related to the student's learning program. The master teacher may also be a tutor for particular students when his competence is pertinent to their program requirements.

## Contract Learning

With one or more master teachers available to work with students in this fashion, an institution can begin to provide opportunities for contract learning for the development of individually planned and supervised programs of study. Few persons have had much experience with this approach to teaching and learning. General criteria that distinguish sound contracts from the unsound ones have yet to be well articulated and none have been examined by any kind of systematic research.

There is more agreement about the structural aspects of a sound contract than there is about how effective judgements concerning substance can be made. John McCormick, a former Empire State colleague, helped me prepare a working paper which summarized the comments of several faculty members who constituted the Committee on Academic Quality, charged with the task of developing guidelines for Empire State's learning contracts. The committee members recognized that these comments were only a minimal beginning, and they are currently trying to move beyond structural considerations into the difficult issues of substance. The initial reactions are worth sharing with others who have not yet tested this new approach.

Several generalizations which emerge from the committee report begin to describe guidelines by which contracts can be judged. There is no guarantee that the actual behavior of the student and mentor will be consistent with the plans specified, nor is there any guarantee that learning will occur even if the activities are pursued. It is reasonable to assume, however, that fruitful activity which results in learning is more likely to occur when a contract conforms to the following guidelines than when it does not.

*Student Purposes and Background.* A contract should make explicit the student's long-range objectives and the purposes to be served by the activities specified. If the contract has been influenced by assumptions concerning special abilities or weaknesses, particular assets or liabilities which arise out of the student's background or prior educational experiences or which are a function of his or her current situation, those assumptions also should be made explicit. The appropriateness of the study plan to the purposes, the background, and the life of the student should be apparent. Later contracts should build on the work and evaluations of previous ones and make these relationships clear.

*Clear and Coherent Organization.* A contract should indicate clearly what is to be done, why it is being done, how it is to be done, how it is to be judged, and a realistic time span for the work. Field work is identified and the arrangements for supervision and evaluation are described. The bibliography is complete and clear. The timing and purposes of appointments with mentors and others are specified.

*Diversity and Variety.* A contract should include a variety of learning activities and resources. It is pluralistic in the views it presents concerning social, personal, or intellectual issues. Human contact and exchange, field experiences and work activities, films, radio and television, all can equal or surpass print in educational power, and the chance of significant learning increases with the range of stimuli and processes a student experiences. A contract should make explicit use of periods of reflection and provide arrangements so that can occur.

*Integration.* A contract should indicate the relationships between readings, writings, and field work. It provides for, and makes clear, links between theory and application. The interdisciplinary nature of knowledge is recognized. It strikes a balance between feelings and intellect, means and ends, inner and outer behaviors.

*Expansion and Continuity.* A contract should be forward looking and point out the range of possibilities for further study. It requires a student to use higher mental processes and suggests additional disciplines, areas of study, and further field experiences which are pertinent to the student's purposes and which may be pursued in later contracts.

*Bibliographic Specificity.* Bibliographic references should be selected that are appropriate to the student's background and level of comprehension. The purposes of specific readings or sets of readings should be specified and they should reflect the debates, issues, areas of controversy, within a pertinent frame of reference. Whenever possible, they should help build a bridge between theory and application, from one discipline to another, and reflect historical as well as contemporary views.

*Mentor Role.* A contract should spell out clearly the role and responsibilities of the mentor. The times and purposes of meetings between mentor and student are specified. When the contract includes areas outside the competence of the mentor, the arrangements for consultation, tutoring, supervision, and evaluation are made clear.

*Evaluation.* Evaluation should be integrally built into each contract, with the procedures and criteria clearly described. Conferences between students and mentors are useful for purposes of evaluation, but many other evaluative instrumentalities and procedures can be used, and a good contract includes some of them. (See Empire State College Working Paper, 1972, for the complete analysis and evaluation of each part.)

The mentor, the master teacher, who develops sound contracts that conform to even these basic structural considerations faces a challenging task when he deals with twenty or thirty students of different ages, different backgrounds, different abilities and cognitive styles, even when their educational purposes are closely allied to the teacher's major areas of competence and knowledge. Recall the distinctions between field-dependent and field-independent students, for example. The field-independent student thrives on materials that challenge his analytic capabilities; he wants clear and sharp feedback more than personal support and encouragement. For the field-dependent student, however, warm support and frequent encouragement are important. Middle class, intellectually oriented students with successful academic careers behind them, trained to work toward long range goals, must be clearly distinguished from disadvantaged or working class students who will need a very different kind of contract. Moore (1970, pp. 104, 136, 137) suggests some of the differences in his analysis of high-risk students:

> High-risk students develop security and confidence when they know specifically what to do and how to do it; more specifically, when a student knows what is expected of him and he has been taught how to perform, he feels that he can succeed. He becomes more secure because he does not have to guess what is wanted and he is more confident if he has been provided with the right prescription for success.
>
> High risk students learn best when they are involved with the learning process. This means, for example, that the teaching technique used to teach the student cannot always be a monologue (lecture); most of the time the teaching method should be a dialogue (seminars, discussion, and so on), or a climate where the

learner can act, react, and interact with the material to
be learned. . . .

High risk students like to see immediate success.
The success might be small but immediate gratification is
the hallmark of the disadvantaged. They also want to
experience many accomplishments. Each achievement,
however small, reinforces the desire for and approach to
the next task. In fact, these students prefer many continuous small successes to a few large ones. . . . High
risk students respond in a positive way to the individual
attention from instructors and counselors. . . .

Marginal students do not like ideas hidden in a
sophisticated verbal vocabulary, couched in compound
complex sentences, obscured in complicated paragraphs,
and written by professional educators to impress their
colleagues, rather than written to help the student. These
students will not always put *isn't* and *aren't* in the right
place, but they can handle sophisticated ideas. . . . At
the same time, they do not learn efficiently when the
material chosen to instruct them is an insult to their
intelligence.

The master teacher, or mentor, also helps his student work
together with others. By helping each student connect with others
who have similar interests he not only enriches their ongoing academic study and learning, but also helps the student begin to shift
his identification to others, associated with the institution, who may
be more identified with his aspirations and his current problems than
the friends and reference groups that are part of his home community.
These study groups are established and carry on their work in a
fashion very different from the usual course or seminar. The mentor
helps them organize and may serve as a resource person within the
limits of his time and energy. He also helps the group identify and
make use of additional resource persons pertinent to their interests.
But principal responsibility for defining the group's agenda, for
determining its sequence and substance, for identifying the meeting
places and frequency of meetings, rests with the students. The groups
will usually be open to any interested student irrespective of his

mentor, and different students will participate in different ways, varying their attendance and their contribution with their purposes and interests.

These group studies are part of, and not apart from, individually planned contracts. The criteria for evaluating the learning which is part of group studies are made explicit in the individual contracts, and therefore final responsibility for judging the success of the contract of which the group study is a part, rests with the mentor for the individual contract.

Not many master teachers ready to deal with the diverse range of students will be found on most college campuses. To do this job a new kind of professional is required. The typical clinical or counseling psychologist cannot do it. Neither can the typical guidance counselor of vocational placement counselor. These persons do not have sufficient command of the various areas of academic knowledge and competence required, nor do they have experience with the areas of professional or vocational interest which many students bring. To develop a sound educational program with a student requires these areas of substantive knowledge and competence. But it is hard to find persons with the requisite breadth of academic knowledge and professional experience who have the counseling and advising skills necessary for effective exchange with students which involve them seriously in their own education and which also result in sound programs of study. Fortunately, however, neither broad knowledge and competency nor counseling skills are genetically determined. Both can be learned, and many faculty members already have a good start.

It has been found at Empire State that the multiple facets of learning planned in Learning Contracts are especially helpful to commuting students. If it is only possible for a limited number of students to work with master teachers in a plan of contract learning at the outset, by giving first priority to commuting students, whose need is greatest, an institution can begin to close the gap between them and their more fortunate resident peers. As is the case with all the other institutional programs and resources, the immediate demand will be greatest from resident students because they will learn about the possibilities sooner and be better positioned to respond. It would be unfortunate to acquiesce to that demand in a fashion that once again leaves the commuting students farther behind.

## Short-Term Residential Experiences

Despite the disadvantage of the commuter student compared with the resident student, the potentials of college residencies have seldom been seriously examined or effectively exploited. Some colleges operate on the assumption that students should be in residence continually throughout their college careers. Other institutions, commuting colleges, assume that it is sufficient for students to come to class and go home, and that periods of residency are not sufficiently important to warrant creative energy or institutional investment.

It is known, however, that the most potent exchanges occur in situations where persons come to know each other fully. We have seen it happen in college residences, and it is no accident that research on college impacts indicates that most changes in attitudes, values, future plans and aspirations, and intellectual interests occur during the first and second years, as students come to grips with fellow students and college subcultures.

We also know that requiring students to spend large blocks of time in college dormitories throughout their college career does not necessarily make educational sense. The evidence is quite clear that the impact and value of those residence hall experiences tapers off rapidly after the first or second year.

But the proper response is not the complete elimination of residential experiences. The answer lies in building short-term residential experiences explicitly into the educational plans of students, as part of regularly scheduled courses, programed learning materials, and individually designed programs of study. Suppose groups of twenty or thirty students studying history or literature or psychology or music or French—the list can be very long—came together in residence situations where they could eat, drink, talk, sleep, write, read, exchange reports and experiences, uninterruptedly for two or three days, a week, or longer?

Flexible short-term residential periods also create contexts for interdisciplinary exchanges. Suppose physics and chemistry students came together with poets and painters to share information, insights, prides, and prejudices as they spoke to a common issue or two and did so in a context where one life style rubs against another? Suppose less extreme combinations came together within the humanities, the behavioral sciences, the natural sciences? Through intensive exchanges with fellow students from diverse backgrounds, values and attitudes are challenged, a rich mix of new perspectives and ideas appears, possibilities for other areas of work or study become apparent, concepts and understandings would be driven home. Relationships are established where students can pursue joint interests, suggest good books, offer fleshed out suggestions based on their own experiences.

Short-term residential experiences also add a dimension for students who are in similar settings—jobs, volunteer activities, field studies, and so forth. Bring together groups of students who are working in different educational settings. Bring such students together with others who are working in hospitals, mental health clinics, community service activities. Bring students together who are working on problems of pollution, population, consumer protection. Residential periods of sufficient duration to allow for full exchange amplify the intellectual impact of those direct experiences in major ways.

Such residential periods need not be continuous, frequent, nor scheduled on a regular basis. In the typical course, one or two a semester make a great difference. Ad hoc arrangements which respond to particular periods of availability, or which are timed in functional ways related to topics under study, can serve large numbers of students.

Creative energy in this direction not only makes for more powerful intellectual and personal development. It also opens up the possibility of such experiences to many students who cannot take time out for longer periods. It helps close the gaps between those who can afford long residential periods, and those who cannot afford them.

Currently the educational values of residential experiences are available only to the favored few who have enough money and who can afford the large blocks of time away from employment, family, or other responsibilities. Short-term residential experiences, built into the fabric of the curriculum, enable all persons to manage their schedules and commitments so that participation is possible.

The costs can be brought within reach for both students and the college. All students pay a modest fee for these educational experiences, which are a systematic part of their educational program. The income from this fee supports several short-term experiences, and payment of the fee covers the costs for the student. This income or a major portion of it is allocated directly to instructors, departments, or other appropriate units and earmarked specifically for residential experiences. Where residence halls are already available, arrangements of this kind lead to effective and widespread use. Where college residences are not available, inexpensive accommodations can be employed during slack times. The facilities themselves are relatively unimportant. The important thing is simply to get persons together so that exchanges which add so much to learning can be quickly mobilized and sustained long enough to have meaning for each participant.

## Summary and Conclusion

The recommendations elaborated above are simple and straightforward:

1. Develop an admission and orientation center which provides preadmission information and assistance and which helps students clarify why they are coming to college, what they want to do, and how they will do it, through initial orientation workshops and through such additional follow-up activities as are required for particular individuals with special problems.

2. Ask each student to submit a program of study, outlining his educational purposes and the work he will undertake to fulfill those purposes, and ask each student to apply for graduation by submitting a description of the work he has completed.

3. Let the curriculum of the institution recognize that both educational content and processes must be relevant to individual differences and that the curriculum is basically what different individuals do to learn what they need to learn, to fulfill the purposes that brought them to the college.

4. Develop student and faculty directories which call attention to the rich pool of human resources within reach of each student.

5. Develop a community resources directory which gives information about the varied organizations, institutions, agencies, and other opportunities for on-the-job experiences, volunteer activities, internships, and field observations which students can formally or informally make a part of their college programs.

6. Develop complex, comprehensive, and open-ended learning programs built of small modules which students and faculty members can combine in diverse ways to respond to different patterns of student ability and interest.

7. Identify several master teachers who can help students plan and carry out individual learning contracts which draw on the diverse institutional, human, and community resources available, and let them begin, giving special priority to commuting students.

8. Make short-term residential experiences an integral part of courses, seminars, programed learning materials, and individually designed programs of study, and charge all students a fee to cover the costs of these educational activities.

These recommendations are neither complicated to understand nor difficult to implement. They can be adopted by traditional institutions and adapted to the special conditions of a particular institution. They can become integral parts of new nontraditional institutions currently on the drawing boards or getting underway. None of them require heavy capital investments or major expenditures of institutional resources. Most can be accomplished by relatively small shifts in the functions and responsibilities of persons and offices currently at work on most college campuses. They represent steps toward change already in motion throughout higher education in the United States; they are responsive to the diverse kinds of new students entering the nation's colleges and universities and to the social conditions that are sending them there.

If these modest changes are undertaken they will be of special value to the increasing numbers of students who will live at home with their parents or in their own private housing while pursuing higher education. They will help close the gap between those who can afford long residence on a college campus and those who cannot. Both these groups of students pay the same tuition yet the educational benefits have been far from equal. These changes in admissions, orientation, program planning, and program review, in curriculum, learning resources, and teaching, and in residential arrangements, will help the commuting students close that gap and help them realize the gains made possible for their resident peers.

More importantly, changes such as these may help us discover a sound middle ground between the all or nothing approach which has characterized higher education in the past. They may help us avoid increasing polarization, where some institutions with sufficient resources and status can serve an elite constituency in a residential setting, while many other less affluent institutions must increasingly become commuter colleges serving the masses a second rate education. If such polarization occurs among institutions of higher education, then the social, cultural, and economic distances that already exist between commuter and resident students will be aggravated, and the development of a pluralistic democracy will become even more difficult to achieve.

# Bibliographic
# Commentary

No systematically organized body of research and theory directly addresses the commuting student, his experiences, and the educational outcomes which flow from them. Most of the references cited in this book report report more general research and theory concerning college influences on student development and the dynamics by which such influences occur.

The landmark volume, which summarizes past research and presents the best thinking up to the time of its publication in 1962, is *The American College,* edited by Nevitt Sanford. This 1100-page book discusses student motivation and student cultures, academic procedures and student performance, interactions between students and teachers, effects of college, and general relationships between higher education and the social context. Any serious student of higher education should know this work; much of it is still highly instructive. The next work of this kind is *The Impact of College on Students,* by Kenneth Feldman and Theodore Newcomb, published in 1969. This book summarizes the output from the research explosion which occurred during the 1960s and presents the major conclusions which can be drawn from those studies concerning the influence of faculty, fellow students, curriculum, residential arrangements, and other key elements of the college environment. These two volumes provide not only the best overviews concerning college influences on student development currently available but also a thorough basis for understanding the problems of commuting students and for developing sound responses to them.

My *Education and Identity,* which received the 1969 Book Award of the American Council on Education, also presents a general conceptual framework for thinking about college impacts on personality development. Drawing on prior research and theory, as well as on a longitudinal study of several different institutions, it postulates seven major dimensions of student change and discusses the influence of institutional size and objectives, curriculum and teaching, faculty, residential arrangements, and relationships with fellow students and student subcultures.

Several additional books offer useful conceptual frameworks and insights pertinent to commuting students. Most of these works rest on comprehensive research efforts and set forth a particular theoretical orientation which takes account of existing literature concerning students and colleges. A. W. Astin and R. J. Panos, in *The Educational and Vocational Development of College Students* (1969), focus on educational attainment and the determinants of career plans and aspirations. *Growing Up in College,* by Douglas Heath (1968), reports longitudinal studies of Haverford students and spells out the elements of the varied sources of influence that operated for them. Joseph Katz's *No Time for Youth* (1968) reports a four-year study of Berkeley and Stanford students which made heavy use of recurrent interviews and is rich in detail. Both the Heath and the Katz volumes, through detailed analyses of particular institutions and their students, offer excellent insights concerning the dynamics of college impacts.

Several other volumes have addressed specific concerns. E. Raushenbush, in *The Student and His Studies* (1964) presents individual case histories which show how various academic studies are influenced by and in turn have an influence on the development of the students pursuing them. *Reference Groups,* by M. Sherif and C. Sherif (1964), and *Student Culture,* by W. L. Wallace (1966), describe how peer relationships and student subcultures influence those who experience or join them. *The Creative College Student,* edited by Paul Heist (1968), brings together research concerning college experiences and educational outcomes for creative students in various college settings. Theodore Newcomb and his colleagues, in *Persistence and Change* (1967), report a twenty-five-year follow-up of Bennington graduates and describe the factors which seem to account for the persistence of attitudinal changes which occurred during the college years. George Stern's *People in Context* (1970) reports multiinstitutional studies of the relationships between student needs and environmental pressures.

These varied references are a rich and wide-ranging sample of some of the most significance research and theory concerning the ways students change during college and the determinants of those changes. Numerous other works could be cited, but readers who digest these volumes will have a solid base for creating effective educational programs for commuting students as well as for their residential counterparts and will find themselves led to more detailed writings pertinent to their particular needs.

# References

ADORNO, T. W., FRENKEL-BRUNSWIK, E., LEVINSON, D. and SANFORD, N. *The Authoritarian Personality*. New York: Harper and Row, 1950.

ASTIN, A. "Undergraduate Achievement and Institutional 'Excellence'." *Science,* Aug. 1968, *161,* 661–668.

ASTIN, A. W., and PANOS, R. J. *The Educational and Vocational Development of College Students*. Washington, D.C.: American Council on Education, 1969.

ASTIN, A., and PANOS, R. J. "Institutional Selectivity and Institutional Outcomes." Paper presented at the meeting of the American Association for the Advancement of Science, 1970.

BARKER, R. G., and GUMP, P. V. *Big School, Small School*. Stanford, Calif.: Stanford University Press, 1964.

BARRON, F. *Creativity and Psychological Health*. New York: Van Nostrand, 1963.

BEARDSLEE, D., and O'DOWD, D. "Students and the Occupational World." In N. Sanford (Ed.), *The American College*. New York: Wiley, 1962.

BEECHER, G., CHICKERING, A. W., HAMLIN, W. G., and PITKIN, R. S. *An Experiment in College Curriculum Organization*. Plainfield, Vt.: Goddard College, 1966.

BLOOM, B. S., and OTHERS. *Taxonomy of Educational Objectives, the Classification of Educational Goals, Cognitive and Affective Domains*. New York: McKay, 1956.

BOWER, E. M. "Personality and Individual Social Maladjustment." In W. W. Wattenberg. (Ed.) *Social Deviancy among Youth*. Chicago: University of Chicago Press, 1966.

**141**

BROVERMAN, D. M. "Generality and Behavioral Correlates of Cognitive Styles." *Journal of Consulting Psychology,* 1964, *28* (6), 487–500.

BROWN, O. H., and RICHEK, H. G. "The Mental Health of Commuting College Students." *Mental Hygiene,* 1968, *52,* 354–359.

BUSHNELL, D. S., and ZAGARIS, I. *Report from Project Focus: Strategies for Change.* Washington, D.C.: American Association of Junior Colleges, 1972.

Carnegie Commission on Higher Education. *New Students and New Places: Policies for the Future Growth and Development of America's Higher Education.* New York: McGraw Hill, 1971.

CHICKERING, A. W. *Education and Identity,* San Francisco: Jossey-Bass, 1969.

CHICKERING, A. W. "Communications—Bedrock for College Governance." *Educational Record,* Spring 1970, 148–153.

CHICKERING, A. W. *The Experience of College Questionnaire.* Saratoga Springs, N. Y., 1970.

CHICKERING, A. W. "Field-Dependence, Field-Independence, and Higher Education for the 70's." Paper presented at the Graduate Record Examinations Board Invitational Conference on Cognitive Styles and Creativity in Higher Education, 1972.

CROSS, K. P. "A Realistic Look at the Future of the Student Personnel Profession." Paper prepared for the Catholic Jesuit Student Personnel Association Workshop, 1972.

DAVIE, J. S. "Satisfaction and the College Experience." In B. Wedge (Ed.), *Psychosocial Problems of College Men.* New Haven, Conn.: Yale University Press, 1958.

DE COSTER, D. A. "The Effects of Homogeneous Housing Assignments for High Ability Students." *Student Housing Research,* Apr. 1967.

DEWEY, J. *Democracy and Education.* New York: Macmillan, 1938.

DRASGOW, J. "Differences Between College Students." *Journal of Higher Education,* 1958, *29,* 216–218.

DRESSEL, P. L., and DE LISLE, F. H. *Undergraduate Curriculum Trends.* Washington, D.C.: American Council on Education, 1969.

DRESSEL, P. L., and LEHMANN, I. J. "The Impact of Higher Education on Student Attitudes, Values, and Critical Thinking Abilities." *Educational Record,* 1965, *46* (3), 248–258.

Empire State College. *Bulletin, 1971–72.* Saratoga Springs, N. Y., 1971.

Empire State College. "Learning Contracts: Working Paper for the

Committee on Academic Quality." Saratoga Springs, N. Y., 1972a.

Empire State College. *Master Plan*. Saratoga Springs, N. Y., 1972b.

EPPS, E. G. "Interpersonal Relations and Motivation: Implications for Teachers of Disadvantaged Children. *Journal of Negro Education*, 1970, *39*, 14–25.

ERICKSON, E. H. "Growth and Crisis of the Healthy Personality." In M. J. E. Senn (Ed.), *Symposium on the Healthy Personality*. Splmnt. 2. New York: Josiah Macy Jr. Foundation, 1950.

ERICKSON, E. H. *Childhood and Society*. New York: Norton, 1963.

FANTINI, M. D., and WEINSTEIN, G. *Disadvantaged Challenge to Education*. New York: Harper and Row, 1968.

FELDMAN, K. A., and NEWCOMB, T. M. *The Impact of College on Students*. San Francisco: Jossey-Bass, 1969.

FREEDMAN, M. B. *The College Experience*. San Francisco: Jossey-Bass, 1967.

FRITZ, R. J. "A Comparison of Attitude Differences and Changes of College Freshman Men Living in Various Types of Housing." *Dissertation Abstracts*, 1956, *16* (11), 2071–2072.

GARDNER, R. W., HOLZMAN, P. S., KLEIN, G. S., LINTON, H. B., and SPENCE, D. Cognitive control: a study of individual consistencies in cognitive behavior. *Psychological Issues*, 1959, *1* (4).

GARDNER, R. W., JACKSON, D. N., and MESSICK, S. J. "Personality Organization in Cognitive Controls and Intellectual Abilities." *Psychological Issues*, 1960, *2* (4), 148.

GEORGE, R. L. "Resident or Commuter: a Study of Personality Differences." Paper presented at the meeting of the American College Personnel Association, 1970.

GRAFF, R. W., and COOLEY, G. R. "Adjustment of Commuter and Resident Students." *Journal of College Student Personnel*, 1970, *11*.

GRYGIER, T. "The Resident and the Commuter." *Journal of the American College Health Association*. 1967, *15* (4), 295.

HEATH, D. H. *Growing Up in College*. San Francisco: Jossey-Bass, 1968.

HEIST, P. (Ed.) *The Creative College Student: an Unmet Challenge*. San Francisco: Jossey-Bass, 1968.

HELSON, H. "Some Problems in Motivation from the Point of View of the Theory of Adaptation Level." In D. Levin (Ed.), *Nebraska Symposium on Motivation*. Lincoln, Nebraska: University of Nebraska Press, 1966, 137–182.

KAGAN, J., MOSS, H. A., and SIGEL, I. E. "Psychological Significance of

Styles of Conceptualization." *Monographs of the Society for Research in Child Development,* 1963, *28* (2), (Whole No. 86), 73–112.

KAGAN, J., ROSMAN, B. L., DAY, D., ALBERT, J., and PHILLIPS, W. "Information Processing in the Child: Significance of Analytic and Reflective Attitudes." *Psychological Monographs: General and Applied,* 1964, *78* (1), (Whole No. 578).

KATZ, J. and Associates. *No Time for Youth: Growth and Constraint in College Students.* San Francisco: Jossey-Bass, 1968.

KATZ, J., and SANFORD, N. "The Curriculum in the Perspective of the Theory of Personality Development. In N. Sanford (Ed.), *The American College.* New York: Wiley, 1962, 418–444.

KELLER, F. S. "Goodby, Teacher." *Journal of Applied Behavior Analysis,* 1968, *1,* 79–89.

KENISTON, K. "Youth: a 'New Stage' of Life." *The American Scholar,* 1970, *39* (4), 631–654.

KENISTON, K., and HIRSCH, S. J. "Psychosocial Issues in Talented College Dropouts." *Psychiatry,* 1970, *33* (1), 1–20.

KILPATRICK, W. H. *Philosophy of Education.* New York: Macmillan, 1951.

KNOELL, D. M. "People Who Need College: a Report on Students We Have Yet to Serve." American Personnel and Guidance Association annual meeting, New Orleans, April, 1970.

KOHRS, E. V. "The Disadvantaged and Lower-Class Adolescent." In J. F. Adams (Ed.), *Understanding Adolescence: Current Developments in Adolescent Psychology.* Boston: Allyn & Bacon, 1969.

KYSAR, J. E. "The Need for Mental Health Programming in the Commuter University." Paper read at the meeting of the American Orthopsychiatric Association, San Francisco, April, 1966.

KYSAR, J. E. "Therapy with the Working-Class College Student." *Journal of the American College Health Association,* 1967, *15* (4), 307–311.

LANTZ, H. R., and MC CRARY, J. S. "An Analysis of Parent-Student Relationships of University Student Commuters and Non-Commuters. *Journal of Counseling Psychology,* 1955, *12* (1).

LEVENSON, E., and KOHN, M. "A Demonstration Clinic for College Dropouts." *College Health,* 1964, *12* (4), 382–391.

LUCHINS, A. S. "Mechanization in Problem Solving: The Effect of Einstellung." *Psychological Monographs,* 1942, *54,* (Whole No. 248).

MAC KINNON, D. W. "The Nature and Nurture of Creative Talent." *American Psychologist*, 1962, *17* (7).

MC CONNELL, T. R., and HEIST, P. "The Diverse College Student Population." In N. Sanford (Ed.), *The American College*. New York: Wiley, 1962.

MOORE, W., JR. *Against the Odds: The High Risk Student in the Community College*. San Francisco: Jossey-Bass, 1970.

MORISHIMA, J. K. "Effects on Student Achievement of Residence Hall Groupings Based on Academic Majors." In C. H. Bagley (Ed.), *Research on Academic Input: Proceedings of the Sixth Annual Forum of the Association for Institutional Research*. Cortland, N. Y.: Office of Institutional Planning, State University of New York at Cortland, 1966, 163–170.

"National Norms for Entering College Freshmen—Fall 1969." *ACE Research Report*, 1969, *4* (7).

NEUGARTEN, B. L., et al. *Personality in Middle and Late Life*. New York: Atherton Press, 1964.

NEWCOMB, T. M., KOENIG, K., FLACKS, R., and WARWICK, D. P. *Persistence and Change: A College and Its Students after Twenty-five Years*. Huntington, N. Y.: Krieger, 1967.

NEWCOMB, T. M., *Personality and Social Change*. New York: Holt, Rinehart, and Winston, 1957.

NEWCOMB, T. M. "Student Peer-Group Influence and Intellectual Outcomes of College Experience." In Sutherland, R. L., Holtzman, W. H., Koile, E. A., and Smith, B. K., (Eds.), *Personality Factors on the College Campus*, Austin, Texas: Hogg Foundation for Mental Health, University of Texas, 1962, 69–91.

NEWCOMB, T. M., and FELDMAN, K. A. "The Impacts of Colleges upon Their Students." A report to the Carnegie Foundation for the Advancement of Teaching, 1968. (See entry for Feldman, K. A. and Newcomb, T. M., in this bibliography.)

NEWCOMB, T. M. *The Acquaintance Process*. New York: Holt, 1961.

PRIBRAM, K. H. The New Neurology and the Biology of Emotion: a Structural Approach. *American Psychologist*. 1967, *22* (10).

RAUSHENBUSH, E. *The Student and His Studies*. Middletown, Conn.: Wesleyan University Press, 1964.

RICHARDSON, L. H. The Commuter College Student's Problem in Synthesizing his Life in a Fragmented Developmental Setting. *Journal of the American College Health Association*. April, 1956, *15* (4), 302–306.

SANFORD, N. *Self and Society: Social Change and Individual Development*. Chicago: Aldine, 1966.

SANFORD, N. "The Developmental Status of the Entering Freshman." In N. Sanford (Ed.), *The American College*. New York: Wiley, 1962.

SANFORD, N. "Factors Related to the Effectiveness of Student Interaction with the College Social System." In Barger, B., and Hall, E. E. (Eds.), *Higher Education and Mental Health*. Proceedings of a conference, University of Florida, Gainsville, 1963, 8–26.

SCHUCHMAN, H. P. "The Double Life of the Commuter College Student." *Mental Hygiene*, 1966, *50* (1).

SHERIF, M., and SHERIF, C. *Reference Groups: Exploration into Conformity and Deviation of Adolescents*. New York: Harper and Row, 1964.

STARK, M. Commuter and Residence Hall Students Compared. *Personnel and Guidance Journal*, 1965, *44*, 277–281.

STERN, G. G. "Environments for Learning." In N. Sanford (Ed.), *The American College*. New York: Wiley, 1962.

STERN, G. G. *People in Context: Measuring Person-Environment Congruence in Education and Industry*. New York: Wiley, 1970.

STOCKWELL, D. S. "Differences in Personality Change of Commuter and Resident Students." Project on Student Development, Plainfield, Vt., 1967.

SUMMERSKILL, J. "Higher Education and Change," Paper prepared for the CJSPA Workshop, 1972.

VREELAND, R., and BIDWELL, C. Organizational Effects on Student Attitudes: a Study of the Harvard Houses. *Sociology of Education*, 1965, *38* (3), 233–250.

WALLACE, W. L. *Student Culture: Social Structure and Continuity in a Liberal Arts College*. Chicago: Aldine, 1966.

WEINBERG, M. S., and RAINS, P. M. "Religion, Familism, and the Commuting Student." Paper read at the American Sociological Association meeting, Boston, 1968.

WHITE, R. H. *Lives in Progress: A Study of the Natural Growth of Personality*. New York: Dryden, 1958.

WHITE, R. W. "Sense of Interpersonal Competence: Two Case Studies and Some Reflections on Origins." In R. W. White (Ed.), *The Study of Lives*. New York: Atherton Press, 1963, 72–93.

WITKIN, H. A. "The role of Cognitive Style in Academic Performance and in Teacher-Student Relations." Paper presented at the Graduate Records Examinations Board Invitational Conference on Cognitive Styles and Creativity in Higher Education, Montreal, 1972.

WITKIN, H. A. Psychological Differentiation and Forms of Pathology. *Journal of Abnormal Psychology*, 1965, *70* (5), 317–336.

WITKIN, H. A., DYK, R. B., FATERSON, H. F., GOODENOUGH, D. R., and KARP, S. A. *Psychological differentiation.* New York: Wiley, 1962.

WITKIN, H. A. *Personality Through Perception: An Experimental and Clinical Study.* Westport, Conn.: Greenwood, 1954.

# Index

## A

Admissions: open, 21-22; recommendations for, 107-113, 134
ADORNO, T. W., 94
Adults as new students, 16
Advanced placement testing, 24-25
Alabama, University of, New College at, 30
American Council on Education: freshman survey of, 52, 59-60, 61, 62, 64, 70; Office of Research, xi-xii, 45, 56; Psychological Examination, 93
ASTIN, A. W., xi, xii, 42, 56, 138
Attitudes related to residential status, 49, 66-67, 69, 71-72, 75-79, 82
Attrition, 101

## B

BARRON, F., 94
BEARDSLEE, D., 42
BEECHER, G., ix
Behavior, residential status related to, 66-67, 69, 82-84
BENEZET, L., 17-18, 117-118
BIDWELL, C., ix
BLOOM, B. S., 93
BOWER, E. M., 120
BOYER, E., 18, 19
BROVERMAN, D. M., 94
BUSHNELL, D. S., 22-23

## C

California, University of, Berkeley, 24, 138
Carnegie Commission on Higher Education, xi, 21, 70

Cognitive styles related to matching college to student, 94-101
Colleges: changes in, 23-30; experiences in, 53-63; impact of, 42-44, 132; selectivity of, 56-59; student match with, 86-104; traditional, 3-4
Community College of Vermont, 30, 115
Community colleges. See Two-year colleges
Commuting students: change in, 42-43; characteristics of, 38-41, 45-52; college experiences of, 54-55, 61-63; educational consequences for, 65-70, 71-72, 73-85; increase of, 2; recommendations for, 112, 120-121, 122, 131-132; and reference groups, 89-90
Competence, residential status related to, 68-69, 85
Computer-based education, 34
Contract, 32-33
Contract learning: field-dependence and field-independence related to, 98-100; recomendations for, 126-132, 135
Credit by examination, 24-26
CROSS, K. P., 12-13
Curriculum: individualized, 26-29; new, 21-36; recommendations for, 114-121, 134; relevance of, 116-120

## D

DAVIE, J. S., 86-87
DAVIS, F., ix
DE COSTER, D. A., ix

**148**